A Basic Course

in American Sign Language

TOM HUMPHRIES
CAROL PADDEN
TERRENCE J. O'ROURKE

ILLUSTRATED BY FRANK A. PAUL

T·J·PUBLISHERS

FRANK ALLEN PAUL

is a native Californian, now residing in San Diego. Mr. Paul received his art training at California State University, Northridge and at Otis and Chouinard Art Schools. Fluent in sign language, he has worked as an interpreter for the deaf but now specializes in book design and illustration within the field of sign language publication. He also has worked as research illustrator with Dr. Ursula Bellugi, Director of the Laboratory for Language and Cognitive Studies at the Salk Institute in La Jolla, California, well known for its extensive research on American Sign Language.

Mr. Paul has established himself as *the* outstanding sign language illustrator in the country today. He has illustrated numerous publications including *A Basic Vocabulary: American Sign Language for Parents and Children* by Terrence J. O'Rourke; *Signs of Sexual Behavior* by James Woodward; *American Sign Language: A Look at its History, Structure and Community* by Charlotte Baker and Carol Padden all published by T.J. Publishers; and the highly acclaimed text by Edward Klima and Ursula Bellugi, *The Signs of Language* published by Harvard University Press. He is also known for his work with the National Association of the Deaf and Joyce Media.

Copyright 1980 by T.J. Publishers, Inc.

Published by T.J. Publishers, 817 Silver Spring Ave., Silver Spring, Md. 20910

First Printing October 1980
Second Printing April 1981
Third Printing August 1981
Fourth Printing September 1981
Fifth Printing, December 1981

Library of Congress Number 80-53994

ISBN 0-932666-10-8

ACKNOWLEDGEMENTS

The efforts and support of many people went into the production of this book. We would like to thank the following for their ideas, criticisms, and suggestions on how to make this book useful for teachers of American Sign Language: Ben Bahan, Rubin Latz, Ella Mae Lentz, David McKee, Rick Rubin, and Darlene Scates. Also, thanks to Kerry Ancis for her editing which helped to improve the explanations and overall style of the book.

The models for our pictures deserve special thanks. They are: John Canady, Carlene Canady Pedersen, Joe Castronovo, Gil Eastman, Ella Mae Lentz, Dorothy Miles, Freda Norman, and Ken Pedersen. John Canady and Freda Norman, in addition to providing us with a breath of fresh air with their lively presences, were valuable consultants in preparing pictures for the sentences used in the text.

Ben Bahan, Carlene Canady Pedersen, and David McKee served as consultants on the sentences used in the explanations and exercises.

We also thank Cyndy Myers and Merrie Davidson for their patience and humor through a seemingly interminable process of typing, retyping and assembling the first drafts of the manuscript.

And for being a companion throughout all stages of bringing the manuscript to life, we are grateful to Frank Paul. As the illustrator and designer of this book, he constantly searched for and experimented with new and better ways to express our work in a printed form.

And finally, we are grateful for the moral support and encouragement we have received from our families, colleagues, and friends.

T.J.O.
T.H.
C.P.

SIGN LANGUAGE MODELS

John Canady   Joe Castronovo   Gil Eastman   Ella Lentz

Dorothy Miles   Freda Norman   Carlene Pedersen   Ken Pedersen

TABLE OF CONTENTS

INTRODUCTION

In recent years, we have seen an upsurge of interest in the sign language used by Deaf people in America. An important factor in this interest is the growing body of research on sign language structure. These research studies have been of immense value in providing new facts about American Sign Language and other foreign sign languages to thousands of people, both Deaf and Hearing. These studies, important as they were to the fields of linguistics, sociology, psychology, anthropology and other sciences, were not intended to be used directly in the teaching of American Sign Language. Clearly there is a need for a language textbook in American Sign Language for adult, second language learners. This book is designed to meet that need. Incorporated into this book are brief explanations and examples of some basic structures of American Sign Language and some exercises for the student to practice these structures.

There are obvious problems with writing a text for a visual-gestural language. This text attempts to alleviate some of these problems by using illustrations and scripts for signed sequences. It should be clear, however, that attempting to learn a visual-gestural language from a textbook alone is no more advisable than attempting to learn a spoken language from a textbook alone. There is no substitute for a visual or spoken model of a language, and for this reason, this book is intended for use with a teacher as well as other teacher-designed activities.

There are a number of other considerations in the use of this textbook which are detailed in the following pages.

AMERICAN SIGN LANGUAGE

The term "sign language" has been used as a generic term for different varieties of sign communication. But there is a significant distinction between American Sign Language and other varieties of sign communication which follow the structure of English.

American Sign Language (also called ASL or Ameslan) is not based on, nor is it derived from English. It is different in structure from the systems which code English or are heavily influenced by English such as Sign English or Pidgin Sign English. ASL is not universal; users of British Sign Language, Italian Sign Language, the Sign Language of India, Chinese Sign Language or many other Sign Languages would not readily comprehend American Sign Language. Both in vocabulary and aspects of their structure, these Sign Languages are quite different from each other.

American Sign Language is the native language of thousands of Deaf people who have Deaf parents. For them, it is not only a first language but also carries with it the culture of generations of Deaf people in America. American Sign Language is also the primary language of many Deaf people in America and Canada who do not have Deaf parents but who nevertheless are members of a sizeable Deaf culture. American Sign Language serves as the principal identifying characteristic of members of this culture and embodies the values and experiences of its users.

Although this textbook gives insight into the language and the culture, a true appreciation of both comes only through association with Deaf people themselves coupled with study. For those who wish to study further, we have provided references elsewhere in this text as guidance.

THE TEXT

The text is composed of twenty-two lessons each of which contains two to four basic explanations of the language structures to be learned. These explanations are clearly marked in the text by means of boxes. In each box are examples and illustrations to explain the structure of the language.

As a resource for the student, a drill or exercise follows each box. These exercises are designed for practice of the language structures to be learned.

At the end of each lesson is a vocabulary section containing the vocabulary used in that lesson as well as other related vocabulary items.

Spaced at intervals throughout the text are several short dialogues which review the language structures discussed in the preceding lessons.

DRILLS AND EXERCISES

The exercises are of several types commonly found in second language learning texts: substitution drills, transformation drills, and question-response drills. Substitution drills usually call for the student to substitute a single sign for another sign in a given sentence keeping the original sentence pattern. Transformation drills usually require a change from one sentence type to another sentence type (i.e., change a statement to a question). Question-response drills require the student to respond to a question asked by the teacher or another student. In all cases, the drills are to be signed, not written. The text is to be used only as a script for practice with the structures to be learned. Furthermore, no other language need be involved in any of the drills; practice is always in manipulating or changing one American Sign Language structure into another American Sign Language structure. Answers to the exercises are located in the Answer Key at the end of the text.

The teacher can develop additional exercises and activities where more practice in the structures is needed.

VOCABULARY

Many of the vocabulary items are included in the examples and exercises of the lessons. Although there are nearly 1,000 vocabulary items, the teacher may want to introduce other signs during the course of a lesson which are not included in the text.

The student should be aware that while one sign (for example, WHEN) is acceptable for one geographical region, a different sign is used in another region. We have included a few regional variations on some signs, but not all possible regional variations are included. The teacher may supplement the vocabulary sections with additional signs which are more appropriate to the local region.

The vocabulary sections are intended primarily for review purposes and the student should not attempt to learn any signs from an illustration without at some point seeing a model using the sign in some context.

DIALOGUES

In learning any language, conversational context is important. For this reason, several dialogues have been provided for this conversational practice. The dialogues are based on common situations found in the Deaf culture or within the deaf community. The student should first see the dialogues signed by the teacher or another model. The dialogues as they appear in the text should only be used as scripts (as with the exercises) to help the student memorize the lines in acting out the dialogues. In addition to providing a context and cultural insights, the dialogues can be used to develop a conversational articulation and fluency. Translations for the dialogues can also be found in the Answer Key.

GLOSSES (Writing system)

The sign

could just as well be represented in the text by ⊖, but since this would require that the student learn a new orthography in addition to learning a new language, we have chosen to use capitalized English words to represent the sign translated as 'gas'. Note that the use of the English word, GAS, in capitalized letters is only a *symbol*. Do not be misled into thinking that the English use of the word, 'gas', is fully equivalent to the American Sign Language use of the sign GAS. As an example of the difference, the sign GAS is typically used for automobile or fuel gas, but not natural gas used in stoves or heaters—the fingerspelled sign #GAS is used for the latter.

The use of English to represent American Sign Language signs is simply a convention which we will adopt until a full writing system for American Sign Language is developed. The use of English symbols to transcribe American Sign Language sentences is intended as an aid to the student. These transcriptions or "scripts" are *not* English sentences.

The following conventions are used:

1. A capitalized word represents a single American Sign Language sign.
   Example: HAPPY

2. Several capitalized words joined together by hyphens represent a single American Sign Language sign.
   Example: DON'T-KNOW

3. Letters joined together by hyphens represent a fingerspelled word or abbreviation.
   Example: M-A-R-Y, T-T-Y
4. A capitalized word preceded by the symbol, #, represents a fingerspelled sign.
   Example: #JOB

5. The symbol, + +, indicates that the preceding sign is reduplicated.
   Example: TREE + +
6. The symbol, ~, between two signs indicates that the two signs are blended together in a smooth movement.
   Example: SEE ~NONE

7. The symbol, CL:, represents a classifier sign.
   Example: CL:F

A symbol such as CL:CC indicates that the classifier uses two hands.
Example: CL:CC

We have used some arbitrary characters with the classifier symbol. They are:
   Arrows are used to show orientation of the palm or direction of movement of the sign.
   ** is used to represent bent fingers.
   ° represents extended thumb.
   ⚡⚡ represents wiggling fingers.

TRANSLATIONS

Each American Sign Language sentence as it appears in the text or later in the Answer Key has an English translation. It should be noted that although one possible translation is given, this is not meant to imply that other translations are not possible. Translation from one language to another is dependent on many factors, not the least of which is context. In the absence of context, some translations in the text may be very limited in terms of the full potential of a sentence. The full range of possible translations should always be discussed with the teacher.

Personal Pronouns

1. The handshape for personal pronouns is the pointing index finger.
2. The locations for personal pronouns are:

I, me	WE, us

YOU	YOU-PL.

The signer looks directly at the other person.

HE/SHE/IT, him,her	THEY, them

If the person or object is visible or nearby, the
signer points in the direction of that person or
object. If the person or object is not present,
the signer can point to a location on either side.

Exercise 1.1:

Change the pronoun form from singular to plural, or from plural to singular.

EXAMPLES:

A. I
    WE
B. THEY
    HE/SHE/IT

1. YOU	4. THEY	7. HE
2. SHE	5. IT	8. I
3. WE	6. YOU-PL.	

Basic Sentence Structure: Sentences with Predicate Adjectives

1. It is common in simple sentences to repeat the subject pronoun at the end of the sentence.

EXAMPLES:

A. I HAPPY I. 'I am happy.'

B. SHE TIRED SHE. 'She is tired.'
C. HE SMART HE. 'He is smart.'

2. The following two forms are possible also:

EXAMPLES:

A. I HAPPY. 'I am happy.'

B. HAPPY I. 'I am happy.'

Exercise 1.2:

Following the example given, form new sentences from the pronouns and adjectives listed below.

EXAMPLE:

I, HAPPY
   I HAPPY I. 'I am happy.'
   I HAPPY. 'I am happy.'
   HAPPY I. 'I am happy.'

1. YOU, TALL
2. IT, HEAVY
3. I, SURPRISED
4. THEY, DEAF
5. YOU, HEARING
6. I, MAD
7. SHE, SLEEPY
8. WE, DEAF
9. IT, LIGHT
10. YOU, HAPPY
11. WE, SURPRISED
12. HE, INTERESTING
13. YOU, PRETTY
14. IT, UGLY

8

15. I, SHORT
16. THEY, SURPRISED
17. IT, BIG

18. I, SLEEPY
19. IT, SMALL
20. SHE, DEAF

Vocabulary

AND

ANGRY, furious

BEAUTIFUL

BIG, large

COOL, breeze

DEAF

DEAF

DUMB, stupid

HAPPY

HARD-OF-HEARING

HE,SHE,IT, him, her

HEARING, SAY, speech

HEAVY

HELLO, hi

I, me

INTERESTING, interest

LIGHT (weight)

MAD, angry

PRETTY, beautiful

SAD

SHORT (height), small

SLEEPY, drowsy   SMALL, little   SMART, clever, bright

STRONG, strength, powerful   STUPID, ignorant, dumb   SURPRISED, amazed

TALL   TALL   THEY, them

TIRED, exhausted   UGLY   WARM

11

WE, us

WEAK, weakness

YOU

YOU-PL.

NOTES

LESSON 12

Possessives

The handshape for possessives is the 5-hand, fingers together. The locations are the same as personal pronouns. The palm moves in the direction of the "owner."

MY, mine	OUR, ours

YOUR, yours	YOUR-PL., yours

HIS/HER/ITS, hers	THEIR, theirs

Exercise 2.1:

Change the personal pronouns listed below to possessives.

EXAMPLE:

I
   MY

1. YOU
2. SHE
3. WE
4. THEY
5. YOU-PL.

6. IT
7. ME
8. HE
9. HIM
10. THEM

Basic Sentence Structure: Sentences with Identifying Nouns

Simple sentences with nouns which identify the subject (predicate nominatives) are commonly structured like the simple sentences with predicate adjectives. The subject pronoun can be repeated at the end of the sentence.

EXAMPLES:

A. SHE TEACHER SHE.   'She is a teacher.'

B. SHE STUDENT.   'She is a student.'
C. MY MOTHER SHE.   'She is my mother.'

Exercise 2.2:

Following the example given, form new sentences from the following list.

˙EXAMPLES:

A. MY, MOTHER
　　　SHE MY MOTHER.　'She is my mother.'
B. WOMAN
　　　SHE WOMAN SHE.　'She is a woman.'

1. MY, SISTER
2. MY, BROTHER
3. YOUR, FATHER
4. OUR, FATHER
5. MY, GRANDMOTHER
6. MY, FRIEND
7. YOUR, GRANDFATHER

8. YOUR, TEACHER
9. MY, STUDENT
10. MY, FRIEND
11. BOY
12. GIRL
13. MAN
14. WOMAN

Using Two-Third Person Pronouns

When the sentence refers to two different persons such as HE and SHE, or HE and HE (meaning another person), point to two different locations for the different persons. Remember that if the persons are not present, the signer can refer to one person on one side of the signer and the other person on the opposite side.

EXAMPLE:

HE HIS TEACHER HE.　'He is his teacher.'

Exercise 2.3:

Following the example given, form new sentences from the pronouns and nouns listed below.

EXAMPLE:

HER, BROTHER
    HE HER BROTHER HE.   'He is her brother.'

1. HER, SISTER
2. HER, MOTHER
3. SHE, THEIR, TEACHER
4. HIS, GRANDMOTHER
5. HER, FRIEND

6. HIS, STUDENT
7. HE, HER, BROTHER
8. HIS, FATHER
9. HER, GRANDFATHER
10. SHE, HIS, SISTER

NOTE: Use of AGENT Suffix

As with TEACHER and STUDENT, the AGENT suffix can be added to a sign to indicate profession or identity.

EXAMPLES: Profession

A. DANCER (DANCE + AGENT)	B. COOK (COOK + AGENT)

EXAMPLE: Identity

C. AMERICAN (AMERICA + AGENT)

Vocabulary

AMERICA

AUNT

BOY, man

BROTHER

CHILD, short

COOK, bake

DANCE, party

DAUGHTER

FAMILY

FATHER

FRIEND

GIRL

GOOD-FRIEND

GRANDFATHER

GRANDMOTHER

HIS, HERS, ITS

HUSBAND

LEARN, acquire

MAN

MOTHER

MY, mine

NEPHEW

NIECE

OUR, ours

19

PARENTS

 PLEASE

 SISTER

 SON

 STUDENT

 TEACH, educate

 TEACHER

 THEIR, theirs

 UNCLE

 WIFE

 WOMAN

YOUR, yours   YOUR-PL., yours

LESSON 3

Basic Sentence Structure: Sentences with Verbs

A common sentence structure with verbs is Subject + Verb + Object.

EXAMPLES:

A. I HAVE BOOK I. 'I have a book.'

B. HE NEED MONEY HE. 'He needs money.'
C. SHE WANT CAR SHE. 'She wants a car.'

Exercise 3.1:

Using the example given, substitute verbs from the list below.

EXAMPLE:

I HAVE BOOK I. 'I have a book.'
NEED
   I NEED BOOK I. 'I need a book.'

1. FORGET
2. REMEMBER
3. LIKE
4. KNOW

5. WANT
6. HAVE
7. READ
8. LOSE

9. FIND
10. ENJOY

Basic Sentence Structure: Pronouns and Nouns

Pronouns are often used together with nouns. In these cases, the pronoun functions like the English word, <u>the</u>. The pronoun can occur either before or after the noun.

EXAMPLES:

A. MAN HE KNOW ME HE.   'The man knows me.'

B. SHE WOMAN HAVE MY BOOK SHE.   'The woman has my book.'

EXERCISE 3.2:

Using the example given, substitute signs from the list below.

EXAMPLE:

MAN HE KNOW ME HE.   'The man knows me.'
  WOMAN
    <u>WOMAN</u> SHE KNOW ME SHE.   'The woman knows me.'
  LIKE
    WOMAN SHE <u>LIKE</u> ME SHE.   'The woman likes me.'
  BOOK
    WOMAN SHE LIKE <u>BOOK</u> SHE.   'The woman likes the book.'

23

1. REMEMBER	11. MAN
2. YOUR NAME	12. PRACTICE
3. FORGET	13. WOMAN
4. BOOK	14. HAVE, CHAIR
5. BOY	15. NEED
6. HAVE	16. CAR
7. PAPER	17. MAN, MONEY
8. NEED	18. WANT
9. GIRL	19. GIRL, BOOK
10. REMEMBER, SIGN	20. HAVE

Basic Sentence Structure: Adjectives and Nouns

Adjectives appear either before or after the noun.

EXAMPLES:

A. I WANT BOX RED I.   'I want a red box.'

I WANT RED BOX I.   'I want a red box.'

B. I REMEMBER CAR BLUE I.   'I remember a blue car.'
   I REMEMBER BLUE CAR I.   'I remember a blue car.'

Exercise 3.3:

To the following sentences add the adjective following the noun.

EXAMPLE:

I HAVE CAR I.   'I have a car.'
  (BLUE)
    I HAVE CAR BLUE I.   'I have a blue car.'

1. I READ BOOK.   (INTERESTING)

2. HE HAVE HOME HE.   (PRETTY)

3. SHE WANT CHAIR.   (BLUE)

4. I REMEMBER MAN.   (TALL)

5. HE LOSE BOOK HE.   (GREEN)

6. THEY FIND BOX.   (SMALL)

7. HE WANT TABLE.   (NEW)

8. I NEED PAPER FOR CLASS I.   (YELLOW)

9. I KNOW WOMAN I.   (DEAF)

10. SHE LIKE CAR SHE.   (SMALL)

Exercise 3.4:

Repeat Exercise 3.3 with the adjective before the noun.

EXAMPLE:

I HAVE CAR I.   'I have a car.'
  (BLUE)
    I HAVE BLUE CAR I.   'I have a blue car.'

Descriptive Adjectives

There are some signs called <u>classifiers</u> which identify and describe an object by representing its size and shape. These classifiers can change to show the relative size of objects.

CL:F

For small, flat and round objects such as a coin, a button, a watch.

CL:L̈L̈

For flat and round objects such as a pancake, a small dish or plate, a hamburger.

CL:L̈L̈

For larger flat and round objects such as a large plate, a big steak, a large puddle.

CL:C

For small container-like objects such as a cup, a glass, a bottle, a vase, a can.

CL:CC

For container-like objects such as a bowl, a large can, a thick cable.

CL:CC

For larger container-like objects such as a pail, a large bowl, a hat box.

CL:BB

For objects with a flat surface such as the top of a small table, or a shelf.

CL:BB

For longer objects with a flat surface such as a long board, a long shelf, a long table, a plot of land.

When using sentences with descriptive classifiers, the signer looks at the classifier.

EXAMPLE:

IT CL:F.   'It is small, flat, and round.'

Exercise 3.5:

For the objects listed below, give the appropriate classifier.

EXAMPLE:

'coin'
　　IT CL:F.   'It is small, flat, and round.'

1. 'long sheet of paper'
2. 'tortilla'

3. 'round mint'
4. 'unfolded map'

5. 'fabric on floor'
6. 'platter'
7. 'beer can'
8. 'manhole cover'

9. 'bucket'
10. 'soap dish'
11. 'cereal bowl'
12. 'Susan B. Anthony dollar'

Vocabulary

ABOUT, concerning

BED

BLACK, Black-person

BLUE

BOOK

BOX, package, room

BROWN

BROWN

CAR

CHAIR, seat

 CLASS, GROUP, team

 COLOR

 DIALOGUE, talk with

 ENJOY, appreciate

 FIND, discover

 FINGERSPELL

 FOR

 FORGET

 FROM

 GRAY

 GREEN

29

HAVE, own, possess   HOME   IN, contained in

KNOW, aware, conscious   LIKE   LOSE

MONEY, financial, economic   NAME   NEED, necessary

NEW, modern   OLD, age   ORANGE

PAPER, page

PRACTICE, exercise, train, rehearse

READ

RED

REMEMBER

SIGN, sign language

TABLE, desk

THANK-YOU

WANT, desire

WHITE

WHITE-PERSON

YELLOW

Negatives

There are several ways to form negative sentences. All are accompanied by a negative marker, _____ n _____ , which is:
1. a headshake
2. eyebrows squeezed together

The different forms of negative sentences are:

1. Use of NOT. NOT either comes before the verb or at the end of the sentence.

EXAMPLES:

```
_____ n _____
```
A. I REMEMBER GIRL NOT I.   'I don't remember the girl.'

```
_____ n _____
```
B. I NOT REMEMBER GIRL I.   'I don't remember the girl.'
```
_____ n _____
```
C. HE NEED MONEY NOT HE.   'He doesn't need money.'
```
_____ n _____
```
D. HE NOT NEED MONEY HE.   'He doesn't need money.'

2. Use of Negative Incorporation. The negative of these verbs, KNOW, WANT, and LIKE, are formed by incorporating an outward, twisting movement.

EXAMPLES:

_____ n _____
A. I DON'T-KNOW WOMAN I.   'I don't know the woman.'

_____ n _____
B. DON'T-WANT MONEY SHE.   'She doesn't want the money.'

_____ n _____
C. HE DON'T-LIKE BOOK HE.   'He doesn't like the book.'

3. Use of Negative Marker. _____ n _____ may be used alone to negate a simple sentence.

EXAMPLES:

___ n _____
A. I READ BOOK I.   'I'm not reading the book.'

_____ n _____
B. I UNDERSTAND MOVIE I.   'I don't understand the movie.'

33

Exercise 4.1:

Change the following sentences to negative sentences by adding NOT or a negative incorporation in addition to the negative marker.

EXAMPLES:

A. I KNOW WOMAN I.   'I know the woman.'
_____ n _____
I DON'T-KNOW WOMAN I.   'I don't know the woman.'

B. SHE FEEL GOOD SHE.   'She feels well.'
_____ n _____
SHE FEEL GOOD NOT SHE.   'She doesn't feel well.'
_____ n _____
SHE NOT FEEL GOOD SHE.   'She doesn't feel well.'

1. HE LIKE MOVIE HE.

2. DAUGHTER SHE LIKE SCHOOL SHE.

3. I SEE DOG I.

4. IT SMELL GOOD IT.

5. I UNDERSTAND BOOK I.

6. THEY BELIEVE YOU.

7. CAT IT HUNGRY IT.

8. HOUSE IT EXPENSIVE IT.

9. IT FOOD HOT IT.

10. WOMAN SHE WANT T-T-Y SHE.

11. SHE KNOW SIGN SHE.

12. BOY HE LOSE MONEY HE.

13. CAR IT BLUE IT.

Exercise 4.2:

Change the following sentences to negative sentences by using only the negative marker.

EXAMPLE:

I REMEMBER YOUR HOUSE I.   'I remember your house.'
_____ n _____
I REMEMBER YOUR HOUSE I.   'I don't remember your house.'

1. I TIRED I.

2. YOU UNDERSTAND ME.

3. GIRL HAVE BOOK SHE.

4. MY SISTER FIND MONEY.

5. I SMELL IT I.

6. I WORK I.

7. THEY PRACTICE SIGN.

Yes/No Questions

Questions that ask for a "Yes" or "No" answer are made by simultaneously:
1. Raising the eyebrows.
2. Moving the head slightly forward.
3. Looking directly at the person being asked the question.

_____q_____ will be used to represent the above grammatical features of Yes/No questions.

EXAMPLE:

Statement: SURPRISED ME.   YOU REMEMBER MY NAME YOU. 'I'm surprised. You remember my name.'

_____q_____
Question: YOU REMEMBER MY NAME YOU? 'Do you remember my name?'

Exercise 4.3:

Change the following statements to questions.

EXAMPLE:

Statement: GRANDFATHER HAVE CHAIR.   'Grandfather has a chair.'
_____q_____
Question: GRANDFATHER HAVE CHAIR?   'Does Grandfather have a chair?'

1. HE LIKE WORK HE.

2. TEACHER LOSE MY PAPER.

3. IT HOUSE COLD IT.

4. GRANDMOTHER FIND MONEY.

5. IT CAT HUNGRY IT.

6. IT BOOK RIGHT IT.

7. DOG IT UNDERSTAND SIGN IT

8. SHE KNOW MY NAME SHE.

9. BOY HE SHORT HE.

10. HE HEARING HE.

Responses to Yes/No Questions

When responding to Yes/No questions, a positive nod of the head accompanies the positive response (represented by _____ y _____), and the negative marker accompanies the negative response. The YES or NO signs may be dropped from the response. The following examples are appropriate responses to Yes/No questions.

EXAMPLES:

_____ q _____
A. HE REMEMBER MY NAME HE?   'Does he remember my name?'

_____ y _____
YES, HE REMEMBER HE.   'Yes, he does.'

_____ n _____
NO, HE NOT REMEMBER HE.   'No, he doesn't.'

_____ q _____
B. SHE NEED MONEY?   'Does she need money?'
_____ y _____
YES, SHE NEED.   'Yes, she does.'
_____ n _____
NO, SHE NOT NEED.   'No, she doesn't.'
_____ q _____
C. SHE KNOW SIGN SHE?   'Does she know how to sign?'
_____ y _____
SHE KNOW SHE.   'Yes, she does.'
_____ n _____
SHE DON'T-KNOW SHE.   'No, she doesn't.'
_____ q _____
D. YOU SLEEPY?   'Are you sleepy?'
_____ y _____
YES, I SLEEPY I.   'Yes, I am.'
_____ n _____
NO, I NOT SLEEPY I.   'No, I'm not.'

There is an additional appropriate negative response to Yes/No questions with predicate adjectives.

_____ n _____
NO, I NOT I.   'No, I'm not.'

Exercise 4.4:

Form appropriate responses to the following questions.

EXAMPLE:

_____ q _____
Question: GRANDFATHER HAVE CHAIR HE? 'Does Grandfather have a chair?'
_____ y _____
Response: YES, HE HAVE HE.   'Yes, he does.'

37

Question	Response
_____ q _____ 1. HE LIKE WORK HE?	NO,...
_____ q _____ 2. TEACHER LOSE MY PAPER?	NO,...
_____ q _____ 3. IT HOUSE COLD IT?	YES,...
_____ q _____ 4. GRANDMOTHER FIND MONEY?	YES,...
____ q ____ 5. IT CAT SICK IT?	NO,...
_____ q _____ 6. IT BOOK RIGHT IT?	NO,...
_____ q _____ 7. DOG IT UNDERSTAND SIGN IT?	YES,...
_____ q _____ 8. SHE KNOW MY NAME SHE?	YES,...
_____ q _____ 9. HE HEARING HE?	YES,...
_____ q _____ 10. BOY HE SHORT HE?	NO,...

Negative Questions

Yes/No questions which contain negatives are made like other Yes/No questions except that the raised eyebrows are squeezed together and a negative headshake is used throughout the question. _____ nq _____ will be used to represent the above-mentioned grammatical features of negative questions.

EXAMPLES:

_____ nq _____
A. HE HAPPY NOT HE?   'He's not happy?'

_____ nq _____
B. YOU EAT YOU?   'You aren't eating?'

_____ nq _____
C. YOU DON'T-WANT CHAIR YOU?   'You don't want a chair?'

Exercise 4.5:

Change the following negative statements to negative questions.

EXAMPLE:

_____ n _____
Statement: HE TIRED NOT HE.   'He's not tired.'
_____ nq _____
Question: HE TIRED NOT HE?   'He's not tired?'

_____ n _____
1. YOU UNDERSTAND ME.

_____ n _____
2. SHE SEE MOVIE NOT.

___ n ___
3. HE DEAF HE.

_____ n _____
4. SHE DON'T-WANT CAT.

_____ n _____
5. HE DON'T-KNOW MY SISTER HE.

_____ n _____
6. IT DIRTY NOT IT.

_____ n _____
7. HE NOT AMERICAN HE.

39

Vocabulary

AWFUL, terrible

BAD, unfortunate

BELIEVE

CAT

CHEAP

CLEAN, NICE, pure

COLD, WINTER

DIRTY

DOG

DON'T-KNOW

DON'T-LIKE

DON'T-WANT

EAT, FOOD

EXPENSIVE

EXPLAIN, describe

FEEL, feelings, sense

GOOD

HEAR, sound

HOT, heat

HOUSE

HUH?

HUNGRY, wish

LANGUAGE

LESSON, COURSE, chapter

LOVE MEET MOVIE

NO NOT OH-I-SEE, oh

RIGHT, correct SCHOOL SEE, sight

SENTENCE, language SICK SMELL, odor

SORRY, regret

TASTE, prefer, favorite

UNDERSTAND, comprehend

WELL, so

WORD, vocabulary

WORK, JOB

WORLD

WRONG

YES

YOUNG, youth

NOTES

DIALOGUE 1

Tom is introducing Betty to Jack.

             _____q_____

Jack: HELLO.   SHE FRIEND YOUR SHE?

       _ y _

Tom: YES.   SHE NAME B-E-T-T-Y S-M-I-T-H.   SHE FROM I-N-D.

Jack: I HAPPY I-MEET-YOU.   MY NAME J-A-C-K J-O-N-E-S.   I FROM M-I-N-N.

                             _____q_____

Betty: HAPPY I-MEET-YOU.   YOU HAVE BROTHER NAME B-O-B

        J-O-N-E-S?

       _ y _   _____q_____

Jack: YES.   YOU KNOW HE YOU?

      _____y___

Betty: I KNOW HE I.

Tom: WELL DEAF SMALL WORLD.

LESSON 5

Basic Sentence Structure: Present and Past Tense

1. The form for present tense is:

I WORK I. 'I am working.'

Also, a tense indicator such as NOW or TODAY may be used either at the beginning of the sentence or at the end of the sentence:

EXAMPLES:

A. NOW I WORK I. 'I am working now.'

I WORK NOW I. 'I am working now.'

B. TODAY I VISIT GRANDMOTHER. 'I am visiting Grandmother today.'
   I VISIT GRANDMOTHER TODAY. 'I am visiting Grandmother today.'

2. A tense indicator may also be used to establish past tense:

EXAMPLES:

A. YESTERDAY I WORK I.   'I worked yesterday.'

B. BEFORE I GO I.   'I went before.'

Among the past tense markers are:

1. RECENTLY   'in the recent past'
2. BEFORE   'in the past, used to'
3. LONG-AGO   'in the distant past'
4. YESTERDAY   'yesterday'

Exercise 5.1:

Change the following sentences to past tense using the tense indicator given at the beginning of the sentence.

EXAMPLE:

I WORK I.   'I am working.'
(YESTERDAY)
   YESTERDAY I WORK I.   'I worked yesterday.'

1. I PRACTICE SIGN I.   (YESTERDAY)

2. HE BUY CAR HE.   (RECENTLY)

3. BOY HE STUDENT HE.   (BEFORE)

4. SHE DIE SHE, SORRY.   (YESTERDAY)

5. I TEACH RESIDENTIAL SCHOOL I.   (LONG-AGO)

6. WOMAN SHE LOSE P-I-N CL:F.   (RECENTLY)

7. $\overline{\text{I NOT READ YOUR}}^{\text{n}}\overline{\text{HOMEWORK.}}$ (YESTERDAY)

8. HE LEARN SIGN HE.   (RECENTLY)

9. SHE HEARING SCHOOL.   (BEFORE)

10. SHE VISIT WASHINGTON SHE.   (LONG-AGO)

Basic Sentence Structure: Using FINISH

It is also possible to use FINISH to show that an action has been completed. FINISH appears either before or after the verb.

EXAMPLES:

A. I FINISH SEE MOVIE.   'I have seen the movie.' or 'I already saw the movie.'

B. I SEE FINISH MOVIE.   'I have seen the movie.' or 'I already saw the movie.'

Exercise 5.2:

Change the following sentences to the past with FINISH.

EXAMPLE:

I BUY CAR. 'I am buying a car.'
  I BUY CAR FINISH. 'I bought a car.'

1. HE FATHER MAKE COOKIE HE.

2. SHE WRITE PAPER SHE.

3. BROTHER READ BOOK HE.

4. I SELL HOUSE I.

5. MOVIE I SEE I.

6. I VISIT GRANDMOTHER I.

7. MY SIGN IMPROVE.

8. HE DRINK WATER HE.

9. SON HE GROW-UP HE.

10. I COOK ALL-DAY I.

Basic Sentence Structure: Future Tense

Among the future tense indicators are:

1. AFTER-AWHILE 'in the near future'
2. WILL 'in the future'
3. LATER 'in the future'
4. FUTURE 'in the far future'
5. TOMORROW 'tomorrow'

EXAMPLES:

A. TOMORROW I GO-AWAY I. 'I will go tomorrow.'

I GO-AWAY TOMORROW. 'I will go tomorrow.'

B. I EAT WILL I. 'I will eat.'

Exercise 5.3:

Change the following past tense sentences to future tense using the future tense indicators given.

EXAMPLE:

YESTERDAY I BUY CAR I.   'Yesterday I bought a car.'
  (WILL)
    I BUY CAR WILL I.   'I will buy a car.'

1. YESTERDAY I PRACTICE SIGN I.   (TOMORROW)

2. LONG-AGO I GO COLLEGE I.   (WILL)

3. RECENTLY I TO-TELEPHONE YOU I.   (LATER)

4. RECENTLY HE LEARN SIGN HE.   (WILL)

5. BEFORE COOKIE CL:ḺḺ I MAKE I.   (FUTURE)

6. T-T-Y SHE BUY SHE.   (AFTER-AWHILE)

7. I SEE MOVIE FINISH I.   (TOMORROW)

8. YESTERDAY PANTS I WEAR I.   (WILL)

9. BEFORE MOTHER STAY 1-WEEK.   (WILL)

NOTE: Establishing the Tense Context

Once the context of tense is established through the use of a tense indicator, it is not necessary to repeat the tense indicator in later sentences until a change in tense is desired.

EXAMPLES:

A. NOW I WORK I.   'I am working.'
    I TEACHER I.   'I am a teacher.'
    I LIKE TEACH I.   'I like teaching.'

B. YESTERDAY I SICK I.   'I was sick yesterday.'
    I STAY HOME I.   'I stayed home.'
    MOTHER SHE TO-TELEPHONE DOCTOR SHE.   'My mother telephoned the doctor.'

C. TOMORROW I SELL MY CAR I.   'Tomorrow I will sell my car.'
    _____ n _____
    I NOT BUY NEW CAR I.   'I'm not going to buy a new car.'
    I WALK WORK I.   'I will walk to work.'

Vocabulary

AFTER-AWHILE, later

AFTERNOON

ALL-DAY

ALL-NIGHT, overnight

BEFORE, previous

BUY

51

COLLEGE, university

COOKIE

DAY

DIE, dead, death

DOCTOR

DRINK

FINE

FINISH, already, then

FUTURE

GO-AWAY, leave

GROW-UP

HOMEWORK

1-HOUR, hour   IMPROVE   LATER

LETTER, mail   LONG-AGO

MAKE   1-MINUTE, minute

1-MONTH, month   MORNING   NIGHT, TONIGHT

NOON

 NOW

 NOW

 PANTS

 RECENTLY, just awhile ago

 RESIDENTIAL-SCHOOL, institute

 SELL

 STAY

 TODAY

 TO-TELEPHONE, call

 TOMORROW

 USED-TO, formerly

VISIT WALK WALK

WASHINGTON (D. C. & WATER WEAR, use
state)

1-WEEK, week WILL, shall, future WRITE

YEAR YESTERDAY YESTERDAY

LESSON 6

Basic Sentence Structure:
Object + Subject + Verb

1. Another common sentence structure is: Object + Subject + Verb.

EXAMPLE:

___t___
IT BOOK GIRL HAVE.   'The girl has a book.'

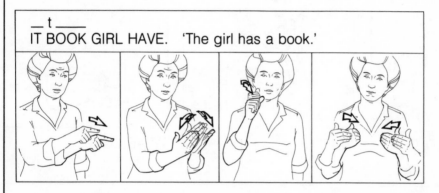

In this sentence structure the object is signed first, and there is usually a topic marker while signing the object of the sentence. The topic marker, represented by _____ t _____, is raised eyebrows.

2. When using adjectives, the following forms are possible:

EXAMPLES:

_____ t _____
COFFEE BLACK SHE LIKE.   'She likes black coffee.'
_____ t _____
BLACK COFFEE SHE LIKE.   'She likes black coffee.'

Exercise 6.1:

Using the example given substitute signs from the list below.

EXAMPLE:

_ t _
COFFEE I LIKE I.　'I like coffee.'
　TEA
_ t _
TEA I LIKE I.　'I like tea.'

1. PREFER	7. BICYCLE
2. HATE	8. DON'T-LIKE
3. WORK	9. MEAT
4. ENJOY	10. NOT EAT
5. T-V	11. SWEET CL:ÏÏ
6. LOOK-AT	12. BUY

Basic Sentence Structure: Directional and Non-Directional Verbs

Some verbs change their movement to indicate the subject and object of the verb—they incorporate the locations of the subject and object pronouns. These verbs are called directional verbs. Some of these verbs are:

SHOW	ASK	TELL	LOOK-AT
HELP	SEND	GIVE	PAY

EXAMPLES:

A. I I-GIVE-YOU MONEY.　'I am giving you money.'

57

B. YOU-GIVE-ME MONEY.   'You are giving me money.'

    C. I I-ASK-YOU.   'I am asking you.'
    D. YOU-ASK-ME.   'You are asking me.'

Note that object pronouns are not signed in sentences with directional verbs except in emphatic forms.

    E. YESTERDAY YOU-ASK-ME I NOT HE.   'You asked me yesterday, not him.'

There are other verbs such as KNOW, HAVE, WANT, NEED, and REMEMBER which do not change their movement to indicate the subject and object, and do not incorporate the location of the subject and object pronouns. These verbs are called non-directional verbs.

    F. I KNOW YOU I.   'I know you.'
    G. YOU KNOW I YOU.   'You know me.'
    H. I REMEMBER YOU I.   'I remember you.'
    I.   YOU REMEMBER I YOU.   'You remember me.'

Exercise 6.2:

Change the following I to you verb forms to you to me verb forms.

EXAMPLE:

_ t __
BOOK YESTERDAY I I-GIVE-YOU.   'Yesterday I gave you the book.'
 _ t __
  BOOK YESTERDAY YOU-GIVE-ME.   'Yesterday you gave me the book.'

   _ t __
1. TICKET TOMORROW I I-PAY-YOU.

```
    _t_
2.  LETTER LATER I I-SEND-YOU.

      _____t_____
3.  RIGHT ADDRESS TOMORROW I I-TELL-YOU.

          _____t_____
4.  TELETYPEWRITER NEW I I-SHOW-YOU WILL I.

5.  I FINISH I-ASK-YOU.

    _t_
6.  LETTER I I-HELP-YOU WRITE WILL I.

7.  I I-GIVE-YOU PICTURE NOW.

8.  AFTER-AWHILE I AGAIN I-ASK-YOU.

      _____t_____
9.  PRETTY CL:ĽĽ I I-SHOW-YOU WILL I.

     ____t____
10. UMBRELLA LONG-AGO I I-GIVE-YOU.
```

Basic Sentence Structure: Directional Verbs Incorporating HE/SHE/IT

Directional verbs also incorporate the HE/SHE/IT pronoun locations.

EXAMPLES:

A. TOMORROW I I-GIVE-HER BOOK.   'Tomorrow I will give her the book.'

B. SHE-GIVE-ME 'she gives me'	C. YOU-GIVE-HER 'you give her'

D. SHE-GIVE-YOU 'she gives you'	E. SHE-GIVE-HIM 'she gives him'

F. HE-GIVE-HER 'he gives her'

Exercise 6.3:

Change the following I to her/him/it verb forms to she/he/it to me verb forms.

EXAMPLE:

    ____t____
UMBRELLA TOMORROW I I-GIVE-HER. 'Tomorrow I'll give her an umbrella.'
     ____t____
   UMBRELLA TOMORROW SHE-GIVE-ME. 'Tomorrow she'll give me an umbrella.'

1. YESTERDAY I I-TELL-HER STAY.

   ___ t ___
2. CLOTHES TOMORROW I I-HELP-HIM BUY.

3. FINISH I I-ASK-HIM WAIT.

   __ t _
4. MOVIE LATER I I-SHOW-HER.

   __t__
5. MONEY TOMORROW IT-SEND-HER.

Change the following you to <u>her/him/it</u> verb forms to <u>she/he/it</u> to you verb forms.

EXAMPLE:

   ____ t _____
UMBRELLA TOMORROW YOU-GIVE-HER.   'Tomorrow you'll give her an umbrella.'

    ____ t ____
  UMBRELLA TOMORROW SHE-GIVE-YOU.   'Tomorrow she'll give you an umbrella.'

   _____ q _____
6. WILL YOU-ASK-HIM WORK?

   _____ q _____
7. BREAD TODAY YOU-HELP-HIM MAKE?

   _____ t _____
8. NEW WRISTWATCH YOU-SHOW-HIM NOW.

   _t_
9. BOX YOU-SEND-HER LATER.

Directional Verbs with Classifiers

Some classifiers can add directional movement and become directional verbs. Two examples of these are:

CL:C	CL:C↑
For small container-like objects such as a cup, a glass, a bottle, or a vase.	For objects which can be held in the hand such as a book, a portable teletypewriter, a stack of papers, a small box.

EXAMPLES:

      __ t __
A. GLASS GIVE-CL:C-YOU.   'I'll give you a glass.'

      __ t __
B. BOTTLE HE-GIVE-CL:C-ME WILL HE.   'He'll give me the bottle.'

----t----
C. TOMORROW TELETYPEWRITER GIVE-CL:C↑-HIM. 'Tomorrow I'll give him
the portable teletypewriter.'

____t____
D. A-B-C-A-S-L BOOK SHE-GIVE-CL:C↑-ME.   'She gave me the ABCASL
book.'

Exercise 6.4:

Use the appropriate C-classifier for the nouns given following the example below.
EXAMPLE:
MILK
_ t _
MILK GIVE-CL:C-YOU.   'I'll give you a glass of milk.'

1. BOX

2. PAPER

3. WATER

4. BOOK

5. GLASS

6. BOTTLE

7. PLANT

8. COKE

Vocabulary

ADDRESS

AGAIN, repeat

ANSWER, respond

ASK

BABY

BICYCLE

BOTTLE

BREAD

CHALLENGE, play
against

CLOTHES, DRESS, wear

COFFEE

COKE

DEPEND

DRIVE

FORCE

FRIDAY

FUNNY, amusing

GIVE

GLASS, CAN, cup

HATE

HELP, aid

INFLUENCE, affect

INFORM, notify, obey

INTRODUCE

LOOK-AT, WATCH

MEAT, steak

MILK

65

MONDAY

PAY

PICTURE, photograph

PLANT, spring

PREFER, rather

PROUD, pride

REQUEST, ask

SATURDAY

SEND, mail to

SHOW, demonstrate,
illustrate

SHY

SUGAR, sweet, cute

SUNDAY

SWEET

TEA

TELETYPEWRITER

TELL

THURSDAY

TICKET

TUESDAY

UMBRELLA

WAIT

WEDNESDAY

WRIST-WATCH

LESSON 17

Imperatives

Imperative sentences, or commands, are made in the following way:
1. The YOU pronoun is usually absent.
2. The signer looks directly at the person being commanded.
3. The verb has a sharp and tense movement. A sharp head nod may accompany the verb.

EXAMPLES:

A. WASH-DISH! 'Wash the dishes!'

_____t_____
B. TICKET YOU-GIVE-ME! 'Give me the ticket!'

Some common imperatives are: STOP-IT, PAY-ATTENTION, COME-ON, GET-AWAY, GO-TO-IT.

C. I I-TELL-YOU FINISH, GO-TO-IT! WASH-DISH!   'I've told you—go and wash the dishes!'

D. NOT LIKE I. STOP-IT!   'I don't like that. Stop it!'

NOTE: The YOU pronoun can be used at the beginning of the command for a more emphatic meaning.

    E. <u>YOU</u> WASH-DISH!   '<u>You</u> wash the dishes!'

Exercise 7.1:

Change the following sentences to commands.

EXAMPLE:

    ___ t ___
PICTURE YOU-SHOW-ME.   'You showed me the picture.'
    ___ t ___
    PICTURE YOU-SHOW ME!   'Show me the picture!'

1. TOMORROW YOU-GIVE-ME MONEY.

    __ t ___
2. LETTER YOU-SEND-HER MOTHER.

    _ t __
3. T-T-Y YOU BUY YOU.

4. YOU PRACTICE SIGN YOU.

5. YOU REMEMBER SIGN YOU.

6. TOMORROW YOU AGAIN YOU-TELL-HER.

7. ADVERTISEMENT YOU-SEND-ME.

8. YOU PAY-ATTENTION YOU.

Using Numbers

1. When counting from 1 to 5 items as in 3 BOOK ('3 books') the palm faces inward to the signer. (The order BOOK 3 is also possible.)

EXAMPLE:

__t__
3 BOOK I HAVE.   'I have 3 books.'

I HAVE BOOK 3.   'I have 3 books.'
I HAVE 3 BOOK.   'I have 3 books.'

2. When indicating age, the sign OLD followed by a number is used. In this case the number is made with the palm facing outward.

EXAMPLE:

SISTER SHE OLD 3 SHE.   'My sister is 3 years old.'

(But not in the order: 3 OLD.)

3. When a number accompanies the sign TIME as in TIME 5 (to mean '5 o'clock'), the palm faces outward.

EXAMPLES:

| A. BREAKFAST TIME 8.   'Breakfast is at 8 o'clock.' |

B. I WAIT UNTIL TIME 5, I GIVE-UP. 'I waited until 5 o'clock, then I gave up.'
(But not in the order: 3 TIME.)

Exercise 7.2:

Substitute the items given into the model sentence.

EXAMPLE:

I FIND 2 BOOK.   'I found 2 books.'
   CHAIR 4
I FIND CHAIR 4.   'I found 4 chairs.'

1. 3 GLASS	3. 5 PENCIL	5. 4 KNIFE
2. COAT 1	4. STAMP 2	6. SPOON 3

EXAMPLE:

TOMORROW BROTHER OLD 3.   'Tomorrow my brother will be 3 years old.'
   OLD 7
TOMORROW BROTHER OLD 7.   'Tomorrow my brother will be 7 years old.'

7. OLD 4	9. OLD 6	11. OLD 5
8. OLD 9	10. OLD 2	12. OLD 1

EXAMPLE:

FRIEND WILL SHE-MEET-ME TIME 2.   'My friend will meet me at 2 o'clock.'
   TIME 5
FRIEND WILL SHE-MEET-ME TIME 5.   'My friend will meet me at 5 o'clock'

13. TIME 9	15. TIME 4	17. TIME 1
14. TIME 8	16. TIME 6	18. TIME 7

Personal Pronouns Incorporating Number

1. There are other forms of personal pronouns that incorporate number:

TWO-OF-US 'the two of us (we)'		TWO-OF-YOU 'the two of you (you, pl.)'	

TWO-OF-THEM 'the two of them (they)'	

EXAMPLE:

TWO-OF-THEM SISTER.   'They (the two of them) are sisters.'

2. The numbers 3, 4, and 5 can be incorporated also:

FOUR-OF-US 'the four of us'		THREE-OF-YOU 'the three of you'	

FIVE-OF-THEM 'the five of them'	

Exercise 7.3:

Substitute the following number-incorporating pronouns into the sentence given.

EXAMPLE:

TWO-OF-US PLAN GO-AWAY. 'We (the two of us) plan to go.'
    FOUR-OF-US
       FOUR-OF-US PLAN GO-AWAY. 'We (the four of us) plan to go.'

1. THREE-OF-US
2. FIVE-OF-US

3. TWO-OF-YOU
4. FOUR-OF-US

EXAMPLE:

THREE-OF-US GO-WITH WILL. 'We (the three of us) will go together.'

5. FIVE-OF-THEM
6. FOUR-OF-US

7. TWO-OF-THEM
8. THREE-OF-YOU

Plurals

There are several ways to make plurals. Two are shown below.

1. Add a number before or after the noun.

EXAMPLE:

I HAVE BOOK 3 I. 'I have 3 books.'

I HAVE 3 BOOK I. 'I have 3 books.'

2. Add a quantifier such as MANY, A-FEW, or SEVERAL before or after the noun.

EXAMPLE:

I HAVE BOOK MANY I.   'I have many books.'

I HAVE MANY BOOK I.   'I have many books.'

Exercise 7.4:

Change the following nouns to plural nouns with the number or quantifier given.

EXAMPLE:

SHE BUY SHIRT SHE.   'She bought a shirt.'
  (5)
    SHE BUY 5 SHIRT SHE.   'She bought 5 shirts.'
    SHE BUY SHIRT 5 SHE.   'She bought 5 shirts.'

1. HE GROW-UP RABBIT HE.   (10)

2. SON HE NEED PANTS HE.   (MANY)

3. SHE ORDER HAMBURGER SHE.   (2)

4. I ORDER FRENCH-FRIES I.   (3)

5. IT STORE HAVE SHOES IT.   (MANY)

6. STUDENT HE HAVE MISTAKE HE.   (A-FEW)

7. SHE FINISH SHE-GIVE-ME PICTURE.   (SEVERAL)

8. I FINISH I-MEET-HER NEW NEIGHBOR.   (SEVERAL)

                    n
9. TWO-OF-THEM NOT HAVE FRIEND.   (MANY)

10. PEOPLE STILL WAIT.   (A-FEW)

74

Vocabulary

ADVERTISEMENT,
publicize, propaganda

A-FEW

AFTER, from now on

BODY

BOTH

BREAKFAST

COAT, jacket

COME-ON

DINNER, supper

EYES

FACE

FRENCH-FRIES

75

GET-AWAY

GO-TO-IT

GO-WITH, accompany

HAMBURGER

HANDS

HARD

HEAD

HEART

KNIFE

LEFT, remaining

LUNCH

MANY, numerous

MIND

MISTAKE, error

NEIGHBOR, next door

NOSE

ORDER, command

PAY-ATTENTION,
concentrate

PENCIL

PEOPLE

PLAN, prepare

RABBIT

SEVERAL

SHIRT

SHOES

SOFT

SPOON, soup

STAMP, postage

STILL

STOP-IT

STORE

TIME

UNTIL, up to

WASH-DISH

DIALOGUE 2

Betty has just been introduced to Jack. Jack finds that she knows his brother.

Jack:
$$\overline{q}$$
YOU KNOW MY BROTHER?

Betty:
$$\overline{y}$$
YES.   I FINISH I-MEET-HIM.   MY SISTER, YOUR BROTHER

TWO-THEM GOOD-FRIEND.

Jack:
$$\overline{n}$$
I DON'T-KNOW YOUR SISTER DEAF.

Betty:
$$\overline{y}$$
SHE DEAF SHE.   NAME SHE M-A-R-Y W-I-L-L-I-A-M-S.

Jack:
$$\overline{y}$$
SURPRISED I.   I KNOW SHE.   BEFORE TIME I SEE SHE

LONG-AGO 6 YEAR.

Betty:
$$\overline{t}$$
M-A-R-Y PICTURE, I HAVE MANY.   I I-CL:C↑-YOU WILL I.

Jack:
$$\overline{y}$$
FINE.   I WANT SEE I.

79

LESSON 8

WH-Questions

WH-questions ask for specific information. These questions use signs such as WHO, WHAT, WHEN, WHERE, WHY, WHICH, HOW, WHAT-FOR ('why'), HOW-MANY/HOW-MUCH. They are made by:
1. Squeezing the eyebrows together.
2. Moving the head slightly forward.
3. Looking directly at the person being asked the question.

_____ whq _____ will be used to represent the above grammatical features of WH-questions. WH-questions use the following form:

_____ whq _____
YOUR CAR WHERE?   'Where is your car?'

_____ whq _____
ICE-CREAM YOU WANT WHICH?   'Which (flavor of) ice cream do you want?'

Exercise 8.1:

Form WH-questions using the statements given.

EXAMPLE:

MAN BUY NEW CAR HE.   'The man bought a new car.'
  WHO
      _____ whq _____
      BUY NEW CAR WHO?   'Who bought a new car?'
  WHAT
      _____ whq _____
      MAN BUY WHAT?   'What did the man buy?'

1. T-T-Y ARRIVE YESTERDAY.
   WHAT:
   WHEN:

2. AUNT LOSE SUITCASE.
   WHO:
   WHAT:
   WHEN:
   WHICH:

3. WIFE NOW SHE VISIT S-D SHE.
   WHO:
   WHERE:
   WHAT-FOR:
   WHY:

4. HORSE IT ESCAPE IT.
   HOW:
   WHEN:
   WHICH:

5. T-V BREAK LONG-AGO.
   WHEN:
   WHAT:
   HOW:

Other Forms of WH-Questions

Other forms of WH-questions are possible besides the form:

———— whq ————
YOUR CAR WHERE?   'Where is your car?'
They are:

1. WH-sign at the beginning of the question:

EXAMPLES:

———— whq ————
A. WHERE YOUR CAR?   'Where is your car?'

———— whq ————
B. HOW YOU KNOW YOU?   'How do you know?'

2. WH-sign at the beginning and the end of the question:

EXAMPLES:

      ————— whq —————
A. WHERE YOUR CAR WHERE? 'Where is your car?'

      ————— whq —————
B. HOW YOU KNOW HOW? 'How do you know?'

3. The WH-marker can be used alone:

EXAMPLES:

    ——— whq ———
A. YOUR NAME? 'What is your name?'

    ——— whq ———
B. EXCUSE. BATHROOM? 'Excuse me. Where is the bathroom?'

Exercise 8.2:

Form WH-questions from the statements in Exercise 8.1 using the forms:

      ————— whq ———
WHO BUY NEW CAR? 'Who bought a new car?'
      ————— whq —————
and WHO BUY NEW CAR WHO? 'Who bought a new car?'

The SELF Pronoun

The SELF pronoun has two functions:

1. It can function as a reflexive pronoun as shown in the following examples:

A. TO-TELEPHONE DOCTOR YOURSELF.   'You call the doctor yourself.'

B. COOKIE I MAKE MYSELF.   'I made some cookies myself.'
C. CHILDREN WRITE LETTER THEMSELVES.   'The children wrote letters themselves.'

2. It can function as another form of personal pronoun as shown in the following examples:

A. MYSELF TIRED, FEEL GOOD I.   'I am tired and don't feel well.'

B. HERSELF WANT BECOME DOCTOR SHE.   'She wants to become a doctor.'
C. THEMSELVES HAVE IDEA MANY.   'They have many ideas.'

Exercise 8.3:

Answer the following questions with the appropriate reflexive pronoun.

EXAMPLE:

_____ q _____
Question: YOU MAKE DRESS YOU?   'Did you make the dress?'
_____ y _____
Response: YES, I MAKE MYSELF.   'Yes, I made it myself.'

_____ q _____
1. PICTURE IT YOUR DAUGHTER DRAW?

_____ q _____
2. YOU YOU-TELL-HIM YOU?

_____ q _____
3. HOUSE YOU CLEAN-UP YOU?

_____ q _____
4. THEY DECIDE WRITE LETTER?

_____ q _____
5. BOOK HE WRITE HE?

_____ q _____
6. HOUSE YOUR FATHER BUILD?

_____ q _____
7. FLOWER YOU GROW YOU?

_____ q _____
8. CAR IT BOY WASH HE?

Exercise 8.4:

Substitute the SELF personal pronoun for the personal pronouns in the following sentences.

EXAMPLE:

___ t ___
COLLEGE SHE WANT GO-AWAY.   'She wants to go to college.'
___ t ___
COLLEGE HERSELF WANT GO-AWAY.   'She wants to go to college.'

1. $\overline{\quad}t\overline{\quad}$ $\overline{\quad}n\overline{\quad}$
   TYPEWRITER I NOT HAVE.

2. HE LONELY HE.

3. SHE HAVE SKILL.

4. $\overline{\qquad\qquad}n\overline{\qquad\qquad}$
   THEY ENTHUSIASTIC STUDY NOT.

5. $\overline{\qquad}q\overline{\qquad}$
   TEST YOU WORRY YOU?

6. $\overline{\qquad}q\overline{\qquad}$
   ANY QUESTION YOU HAVE?

Vocabulary

ANY

ARRIVE

BATHROOM, TOILET

BECOME

BREAK

BUILD, construct

CANDY

CHILDREN

CLEAN-UP

DECIDE, determined, decision

DIFFERENT

DRAW

ENTHUSIASTIC

ESCAPE, run away, get away

EXCUSE

FLOWER

GROW

HIMSELF, HERSELF, ITSELF

HORSE

 HOW

 HOW-MANY, HOW-MUCH

 ICE-CREAM

 IDEA

 LEAVE, depart

 LONELY, lonesome

 MYSELF

 OURSELVES

 QUESTION

 SKILL, ability, expert

 STUDY

SUITCASE, purse

TEST, exam, quiz

THEMSELVES

TYPEWRITER

WASH

WASH-FACE

WASH-IN-MACHINE

WHAT

WHAT, where

WHAT-FOR, why

WHAT-TO-DO

WHAT'S-UP

88

WHEN

WHEN

WHERE

WHICH, or

WHO

WHO

WHY

WORRY, concerned

YOURSELF

YOURSELVES

LESSON 19

Noun-Verb Pairs

There are many nouns and verbs which are related to each other in meaning and form and differ only in movement. These are called noun-verb pairs. Some verbs have a single movement and the related noun has a smaller, repeated movement.

EXAMPLE:

Verb: SIT

Noun: CHAIR

Other verbs have repeated movement and the related noun has a smaller, repeated movement.

EXAMPLE:

Verb: COMB-HAIR

Noun: COMB

Note that while verbs may vary in movement, the related nouns are smaller and repeated in movement. Some examples of noun-verb pairs are:

FLY - AIRPLANE

OPEN-DOOR - DOOR

OPEN-WINDOW - WINDOW

GO-BY-BOAT - BOAT

GO-BY-TRAIN - TRAIN

OPEN-BOOK - BOOK

MEET - MEETING	PUT-IN-GAS - GAS
GIVE-TICKET - TICKET	PUT-ON-HEARING-AID - HEARING-AID
LOCK-KEY	TO-TELEPHONE - TELEPHONE
TELL-STORY - STORY	TO-BICYCLE - BICYCLE
TYPE - TYPEWRITER	GROW - PLANT

Exercise 9.1:

Change the verb forms given in the questions below to their related noun forms in your answers.

EXAMPLE:

         _____ q _____
Question: YOU WANT SIT YOU? 'Do you want to sit down?'

         _____ y __
         YES, I WANT . . .
         _____ y _____
Response: YES, I WANT CHAIR I. 'Yes, I want a chair.'

_____ q _____
1. COP GIVE-TICKET HE?

_____ y _____
COP SHE-GIVE-HIM . . .

_____ q _____
2. WE MEET TOMORROW?

_____ y _____
YES, TOMORROW TIME 3 HAVE . . .

_____ q _____
3. YOU ENJOY TO-BICYCLE?

_____ y _____
YES, I HAVE NEW . . .

_____ q _____
4. YOU FINISH PUT-IN-GAS TODAY?

___ n _____
NO, I NEED . . .

_____ q _____
5. I SEE YOU PUT-ON-HEARING-AID?

__ y __
I HAVE . . .

_____ whq _____
6. TIME I TO-TELEPHONE YOU

_____
TOMORROW?

_____ n _____
NOT TO-TELEPHONE . . . BREAK.

_____ q _____
7. YOU KNOW HOW TYPE?

___ y ___
YES, I HAVE . . .

————q————

8. DOOR YOU FINISH LOCK?   ————n————
                                           I NOT HAVE . . .

9. OPEN-BOOK NOW!   ————n————
                                           I NOT HAVE . . .

————whq————

10. YOU FLY, GO-BY-TRAIN, WHICH?   I WANT . . .

Using Subject as Topic

The topic marker may be used on subjects as well as objects. The marker is used to specify, and in some cases emphasize, the subject.

EXAMPLES:

————t————
A. BICYCLE MY BREAK.   'My bicycle, it's broken.'

——t——
B. HE KID FALL HE.   'The kid, he fell.'

————t————
C. DEAF THEY MEET TOMORROW.   'Deaf people, they are meeting tomorrow.'

Exercise 9.2:

Use topic marking with the subjects in the following sentences.

EXAMPLE:

WIFE HAVE NEW WORK.   'My wife has a new job.'

—t—
WIFE HAVE NEW WORK.   'My wife, she has a new job.'

92

1. GIRLFRIEND HAVE BLOND HAIR.

2. CALIFORNIA WOW NICE.

3. TEACHER SHE-BAWL-OUT-HIM.

4. RAIN STOP.

5. LEADER SHE-ASK-ME QUESTION.

6. HIS WRIST-WATCH STEAL.

_____ n _____

7. TREE IT NOT LOOK GOOD.

8. PERFORMANCE WONDERFUL.

9. PLANT NEED WATER.

10. MEETING CANCEL.

Vocabulary

ACT, perform
Noun: PERFORMANCE

AUTUMN, Fall

BAWL-OUT

BLOND

CALIFORNIA, gold

CANCEL, criticize,
correct

COMB-HAIR
Noun: COMB

COP, POLICE

DOWN

FALL, FALL-DOWN

FLY
Noun: AIRPLANE,
AIRPORT

GIVE-TICKET
Noun: TICKET

GO-BY-BOAT
Noun: BOAT

GO-BY-TRAIN
Noun: TRAIN

HAIR

KID

LEAD, guide

LEFT (direction)

LIBRARY

LOCK
Noun: KEY

LOOK, appearance

MEET (group)
Noun: MEETING,
convention

NOTICE, recognize

OPEN-BOOK
Noun: BOOK

OPEN-DOOR
Noun: DOOR

OPEN-WINDOW
Noun: WINDOW

PERSON

PLACE

PUT-IN-GAS
Noun: GAS

PUT-ON-HEARING-AID
Noun: HEARING-AID

PUT-ON-RING
Noun: RING

RAIN

RIGHT (direction)

SIT
Noun: CHAIR, seat

STEAL

STOP

SUMMER

TELL-STORY
Noun: STORY

THING

TO-BICYCLE
Noun: BICYCLE

TO-TELEPHONE
Noun: TELEPHONE

TREE

TYPE
Noun: TYPEWRITER

UP

WONDERFUL, fantastic, great

WOW

Basic Sentence Structure: Using Modals

The modals that can accompany other verbs in a sentence are: CAN, SHOULD, MUST, WILL, FINISH, MAYBE. There are three types of sentence structure with modals.

1. The modal is at the end of the sentence:

EXAMPLE:

_____t_____
TELEPHONE NUMBER WOMAN SHE-GIVE-ME SHOULD SHE.
'The woman should give me the telephone number.'

2. The modal precedes the verb:

EXAMPLE:

_____t_____
TELEPHONE NUMBER WOMAN SHOULD SHE-GIVE-ME SHE.
'The woman should give me the telephone number.'

3. The modal both precedes the verb and is repeated at the end of the sentence:

EXAMPLE:

_____t_____
TELEPHONE NUMBER WOMAN SHOULD SHE-GIVE-ME SHOULD SHE.
'The woman should give me the telephone number.'

Exercise 10.1:

Use the modal given at the end of the following sentences.

EXAMPLE:

I LECTURE TIME 3 I.   'I lecture at 3 o'clock.'
  (CAN)
    I LECTURE TIME 3 CAN I.   'I can lecture at 3 o'clock.'

1. SHE SEE DOCTOR SHE.   (SHOULD)

   _____ q _____
2. LETTER YOU GET YOU?   (FINISH)

3. TOMORROW PRESIDENT APPEAR.   (MAYBE)

4. HE RECOVER HE.   (WILL)

5. I WIN RACE I.   (MUST)

6. I LIPREAD.   (CAN)

7. LETTER I TYPE 1-MINUTE I.   (CAN)

8. S-F YOU VISIT YOU.   (MUST)

9. HE TAKE-UP MORE CLASS HE.   (SHOULD)

10. SISTER MARRY.   (WILL)

Exercise 10.2:

Do Exercise 10.1 above with the modal preceding the verb.

EXAMPLE:

I LECTURE TIME 3 I.   'I lecture at 3 o'clock.'

  (CAN)
    I CAN LECTURE TIME 3 I.   'I can lecture at 3 o'clock.'

Using Negative Modals

Some negative modals are: CAN'T, NOT-YET, REFUSE.

EXAMPLES:

A. $\overline{\text{I DANCE CAN'T}}^{\,n}\,\text{I.}$ 'I can't dance.'

B. $\overline{\text{I EAT NOT-YET.}}^{\,n}$ 'I haven't eaten.'

C. $\overline{\text{I I-TELL-YOU REFUSE}}^{\,n}\,\text{I.}$ 'I won't tell you.'

Exercise 10.3:

Substitute negative modals for the modals in the sentences given.

EXAMPLE:

I COLLECT MONEY FINISH I.   'I have collected the money.'

$\overline{\text{I COLLECT MONEY NOT-YET}}^{\,n}\,\text{I.}$ 'I haven't collected the money.'

1. I STAY 1-HOUR CAN I.

2. HE ACCEPT RESPONSIBILITY WILL HE.

3. HE FINISH COOK FOOD HE.

4. I GET-UP TIME 6 CAN I.

5. $\overline{\text{TELEPHONE NUMBER}}^{\,t}\,\text{HE MEMORIZE FINISH HE.}$

6. SHE BORN BABY FINISH SHE.

7. MAN HE HE-PAY-ME WILL HE.

      __t__
8. LETTER HE-SEND-ME FINISH HE.

9. I FINISH TRY ESTABLISH C-L-U-B I.

10. ADDRESS SHE PUT-DOWN FOR-YOU CAN SHE.

Using Modals as Responses to Yes/No Questions

The modals can be used as responses to Yes/No questions in the following forms:

Questions:

        _____q_____
YOU DRIVE CAN YOU?

'Can you drive?'

Responses

  __y__
I CAN I.   'Yes, I can.'

  ___n___
I CAN'T I.   'No, I can't.'

          q_____
I BUY BOOK SHOULD I?
'Should I buy the book?'

    ____q____
I PAY MUST I?
'Do I have to pay?'

           y_____
YES, YOU SHOULD YOU.
'Yes, you should.'

           y_____
YES, YOU MUST YOU.
'Yes, you have to.'

       ___q___
I PASS WILL I?
'Will I pass?'

         ___q___
YOU WORK WILL YOU?
'Will you work?'

               ___q___
MEAT YOU COOK FINISH YOU?
'Have you cooked the meat?'

        ___q___
HE PASS MAYBE HE?
'He may pass?'

      ___y___
YOU WILL YOU.
'Yes, you will.'

     ___y___
YES, I WILL I.
'Yes, I will.'

     ___n___
NO, I REFUSE I.
'No, I won't.'

  ___y___
I FINISH I.
'Yes, I have.'

   ___n___
I NOT-YET I.
'No, I haven't.'

     ___y___
YES, HE MAYBE HE.
'Yes, he may.'

Exercise 10.4:

Form appropriate responses to the following questions.

Example:

           ___q___
Question: YOU WORK WILL YOU? 'Will you work?'
         YES . . .
          ___y___
Response: YES I WILL I. 'Yes, I will.'

Question	Response
___q___ 1. YOU-HELP-ME CAN YOU?	NO . . .
___q___ 2. SHE SLEEP NOW SHOULD SHE?	YES . . .
___q___ 3. CAR YOU BUY MAYBE YOU?	YES . . .
___q___ 4. AGAIN TO-TELEPHONE YOU CAN I?	YES . . .
___q___ 5. RESTAURANT HE FINISH ESTABLISH HE?	NO . . .
___q___ 6. POLICE CATCH MAN FINISH?	YES . . .
___q___ 7. PARTY I PLAN SHOULD I?	YES . . .
___q___ 8. RACE HE MAYBE WIN HE?	YES . . .
___q___ 9. TEST TOMORROW SHE TAKE-UP WILL SHE?	YES . . .

Vocabulary

ACCEPT

APPEAR, show up

BAKE, oven

BETWEEN

BORN, birth

CAN

CAN'T

CATCH, capture, arrest

COLLECT

COMPETE
Noun: RACE, SPORTS, competition, contest

CRY

DIVORCE

ENGAGEMENT

ESTABLISH, set up, found

FAIL

FAST

FAULT, RESPONSIBILITY, burden

FLUNK

GET, receive, obtain

GET-UP

LAUGH

LECTURE, speech, presentation

LIPREAD, oral, speech

MARRY, marriage

MAYBE, might

MEMORIZE

MORE, further

MOST

MUST, have to

NOT-YET

NUMBER

PARTY

PASS

PRESIDENT,
superintendent

PROTECT, guard, defend

PUT-DOWN, write down,
record

RECOVER, get well

REFUSE, won't

RESTAURANT

SAVE, preserve

SHOULD

SLEEP

SLOW

TAKE-UP

THINK

TRY, attempt, effort

WEDDING

WIN

NOTES

DIALOGUE 3

Jack is telling Tom about a film made by the National Association of the Deaf (N.A.D.) in 1913.

Jack: I RECENTLY SEE MOVIE INTERESTING. ITSELF OLD MOVIE,

SIGN LECTURE B-Y G-E-O-R-G-E V-E-D-I-T-Z. YOU SEE FINISH

YOU?

<pre>
    ____ n ____   _____ whq _____
</pre>
Tom: NOT-YET I. V-E-D-I-T-Z WHO?

Jack: HIMSELF DEAF, PRESIDENT N-A-D LONG-AGO 1913.

<pre>
    ____ t ____
</pre>
SIGN HIS CAN NOTICE OLD, DIFFERENT.

<pre>
    _____ whq _____
</pre>
Tom: MAKE MOVIE WHAT FOR?

Jack: N-A-D FINISH COLLECT 5,000 DOLLAR, MAKE MOVIE. IT

WANT SAVE, PROTECT SIGN FOR FUTURE DEAF.

<pre>
    ___ whq _
</pre>
Tom: I WANT SEE MOVIE. WHERE?

Jack: LIBRARY HAVE SHOULD. YOU-ASK-IT LIBRARY.

LESSON 11

Adverbials of Place: HERE and THERE

In addition to indicating pronouns, pointing also is used to indicate the adverbials of place, HERE and THERE:

HERE₁

HERE₂

THERE

The direction of the point for THERE is in the actual direction of the referent.

EXAMPLES:

A. MY HOME HERE. 'My home is here.'

B. MY HOME THERE. 'My home is over there.'

110

Exercise 11.1:

Use the following signs in sentences with HERE or THERE. Remember to point in the direction of the referent for THERE.

EXAMPLE:

MY CLASS
    MY CLASS HERE.   'My class is here.'

1. MY HOME

2. YOUR GLASSES

3. CAR

4. COKE MACHINE

5. WOMAN

6. STORE

7. BASEBALL GAME

8. CHURCH OLD

9. PAPER

10. YOUR FRIEND

NOTE: Use of THIS/THAT

1. The sign THIS/THAT can be used as a demonstrative to identify a noun. The location of THIS/THAT is the same as the location of the noun.

EXAMPLES:

    _____ t _____
A. THAT BICYCLE WOW EXPENSIVE.   'That bicycle there is really expensive.'

B. THIS BICYCLE 'This bicycle here'	C. THAT BICYCLE 'That bicycle there'

2. Another related sign: THAT-ONE is usually followed by the pronoun showing the location of the referent.

EXAMPLES:

_____ q _____
A. REMEMBER WOMAN I EXPLAIN, THAT-ONE SHE. 'Remember I explained about the woman? Well, that's her.'

_____ q _____
B. THAT-ONE YOU GOOD-FRIEND MY BROTHER YOU?
'Are you the one that's a good friend of my brother?'

Verbs Incorporating Location

Some verbs change their movement to indicate a change from one location to another. Some of these verbs are:

GO	COME	DRIVE
MOVE	WALK	PUT
BRING	FLY	RUN

EXAMPLES:

To there:

   __ t __
A. FRIEND I GO-THERE VISIT. 'I went to visit my friend.'

B. BEFORE AUTUMN, BOSS MOVE-THERE CHICAGO. 'My boss moved to Chicago last fall.'

To here:

   __ t __
C. FRIEND COME-HERE VISIT. 'My friend came to visit me.'

D. I URGE FRIEND MOVE-HERE S-D. 'I persuaded my friend to move here to San Diego.'

From there to there:

   __ t __
E. FRIEND THERE-GO-THERE VISIT. 'My friend went there (from there) for a visit.'

113

Exercise 11.2:

Substitute the verbs in parentheses into the sentences given.

EXAMPLE:

BEFORE I GO-THERE I.   'I went there before.'
  (DRIVE)
        BEFORE I DRIVE-THERE I.   'I drove there before.'

1. BEFORE I DRIVE-THERE I.   (WALK)

2. BEFORE I DRIVE-THERE I.   (FLY)

3. FURNITURE HEAVY SHE BRING-THERE.   (MOVE)

4. BEFORE YOU COME-HERE YOU.   (DRIVE)

5. BEFORE YOU COME-HERE YOU.   (WALK)

6. BEFORE YOU COME-HERE YOU.   (FLY)

7. BOOK MANY SHE BRING-HERE.   (PUT)

8. CHICAGO, L-A HE THERE-MOVE-THERE HE.   (DRIVE)

9. CHICAGO, L-A HE THERE-MOVE-THERE HE.   (FLY)

10. STORE, YOUR HOME SHE THERE-WALK-THERE.   (DRIVE)

11. STORE, YOUR HOME SHE THERE-WALK-THERE.   (BRING)

FINISH as Conjunction

When used as a conjunction, FINISH means 'then.' It is often used to link sentences occurring in a time sequence.

EXAMPLE:

I DRIVE-THERE BOX SEND FINISH, THERE-DRIVE-THERE FOOD STORE BUY FINISH, DRIVE-HERE HOME.   'I drove there, mailed a box, then drove to the food store to shop for food, then drove home.'

Exercise 11.3:

Combine the following sentences using FINISH as conjunction.

EXAMPLES:

MONEY I-SEND-HIM.   'I sent him the money.'
TICKET HE-SEND-ME.   'He sent me the ticket.'
  MONEY I-SEND-HIM FINISH TICKET HE-SEND-ME.
'I sent him the money then he sent me the ticket.'

1. CHICAGO HE MOVE-THERE, STAY 2 YEAR.

   HE THERE-MOVE-THERE WASHINGTON.

2. C-F NOW I-GIVE-YOU.

   YOU-GIVE-HIM TOMORROW.

3. I STAY-HERE 1-WEEK WITH SISTER.

   I GO-THERE VISIT MOTHER.

4. BREAKFAST I COOK.

   YOU WASH-DISH.

5. SUITCASE I PACK.

   I GO-THERE AIRPORT.

6. PERFORMANCE PRACTICE ALL-DAY.

   TONIGHT HAVE PARTY THERE MY HOME.

Vocabulary

AGREE

ALL

ALMOST

BASEBALL

BASKETBALL

BRING, carry, deliver

CHAT, converse

CHICAGO

CHURCH

COME

DISAGREE

DRIVE-TO

x

117

EMPTY, bare, nude

FAR, distant

FOOTBALL

FULL, complete

FULL, fed up

FURNITURE

GAME

GLASSES

GO

HEADACHE

HEAD-COLD,
handkerchief

HERE

118

HERE

IMPORTANT, worth it, valuable

LIVE, life

MACHINE, engine, factory

MOVE-TO

NEAR, close

NEW-YORK

PACK

PHILADELPHIA

PUT

RUN

TALK, speak

TEMPLE

THAT

THAT-ONE

THERE, over there

THIS

TO-TTY

URGE, persuade

WALK-TO

NOTES

LESSON 12

Existential HAVE

The sign HAVE has two meanings:
1. It indicates possession.

EXAMPLE:

I HAVE MONEY I.   'I have money.'

2. It indicates existence.

EXAMPLES:

A. IT KITCHEN HAVE MILK.   'There is milk in the kitchen.'

B. IT STORE HAVE FOOD IT.   'There is food in the store.'

C. IT HAVE PAPER IT.   'There is paper.'

Exercise 12.1:

Using signs from the following list, form existential HAVE sentences.

EXAMPLES:

A. HOME, COFFEE
    IT HOME HAVE COFFEE.   'There is coffee at home.'

B. RESTAURANT, WATER
    IT RESTAURANT HAVE WATER.   'There is water in the restaurant.'

1. RESTAURANT, FOOD

2. HOME, TEA

3. STORE, SHOES

4. SCHOOL, DEAF STUDENT

5. RESTAURANT, MEAT

6. KITCHEN, TABLE

7. HOUSE, CHAIR

8. RESTAURANT, RESTROOM

9. R-E-F, CREAM

10. BOOK, SIGN

Pronominal Classifiers

Some classifiers can be used as pronouns, that is, they can replace nouns. Three examples are:

CL:3

For vehicles such as a car, a bus, a bicycle, a truck.

CL: ∧

For any person or two-legged animal such as a woman, a child, or a gorilla.

CL:B

For any flat object such as a piece of paper, a magazine, a newspaper.

When used with nouns, these classifiers can show the location of the noun. The noun usually precedes the classifier in the sentence.

EXAMPLES:

   _ t _
A. CAR CL:3-HERE. 'The car is near here.'

B. CAR CL:3-THERE.   'The car is over there.'

C. CAR CL:3-THERE.   'The car is over there.'

Exercise 12.2:

Substitute the appropriate classifier for the HERE or THERE adverbials of place.

EXAMPLE:

I SEE YOUR V-A-N THERE.   'I see your van over there.'
   I SEE YOUR V-A-N CL:3-THERE.   'I see your van over there.'

1. WOMAN THERE, SHE-LOOK-AT-ME.

2. I ENTER, LETTER THERE.

3. SHOULD BICYCLE THERE.

4. SURPRISED ME.   PRESIDENT HERE.

5. CAR BLUE THERE, THAT-ONE HIS.

124

6. SHE FORGET LEFT MAGAZINE THERE.

7. RECENTLY BROTHER HERE, NOW GONE.

8. CAR THERE, NOW PUT-IN-GAS.

Locational Relationships

Pronominal classifiers can be used to show locational relationships such as "on," "under," "behind," "in front of," "beside," "facing each other," "on top of," etc.

EXAMPLES:

'two vehicles next to each other'	'two vehicles, one in front of the other'	'two persons facing each other'

'one flat object on top of another'	'a container on top of a flat surface'	'a container under a flat surface'

Exercise 12.3:

Using pronominal classifiers, indicate the locational relationship of the objects or persons in the following pictures. Use the model sentence given.

EXAMPLE:

I SEE

I SEE CAR CL:3-NEXT-TO-CL:3.   'I saw the two cars next to each other.'

NOTE: Adding Movement to Pronominal Classifiers

The action of persons or objects can be indicated by adding movement to pronominal classifiers.

EXAMPLES:

'one vehicle passing another'	'two vehicles colliding head-on'

'a person diving off a platform'	'a container falling off a flat surface'

Vocabulary

ANNOUNCE, announcement

BURN, FIRE

CREAM

DISAPPOINT, miss

 DREAM, daydream

 EARLY

 EARTH, geography

 ENTER, go into

 GONE

 HURT, pain

 KITCHEN

 KNOW-THAT

 LIE

 LOUD

 LUCKY, delicious

MAGAZINE, brochure,
journal, booklet

MISS

MISUNDERSTAND,
misconception

MOON

NOISE, noisy

POOR, poverty

PROBLEM

PROMISE, commit,
pledge, swear

QUIET, calm, peaceful

RELIEVED

REST

RESTROOM, bathroom

RICH, wealthy

SAME, like, alike

SAME, like, alike, similar

SATISFY, satisfied

SCARE, frighten

STREET, road, way, path

STRICT

SUN

SUNRISE

SUNSET

THIRSTY, thirst

VOICE, vocalize

WAKE-UP

WET, damp, moist

Mass Quantifiers

The quantifiers SOME, A-LITTLE, and PLENTY are added either before a mass noun or at the end of the sentence.

EXAMPLES:

A. HAVE FURNITURE PLENTY I.   'I have a lot of furniture.'

HAVE PLENTY FURNITURE I.   'I have a lot of furniture.'

B. I THINK HAVE LEFT FOOD SOME.   'I think there's some food left.'

I THINK HAVE LEFT SOME FOOD.   'I think there's some food left.'

C. I EAT CHEESE A-LITTLE.   'I'll eat a little cheese.'
   I EAT A-LITTLE CHEESE.   'I'll eat a little cheese.'

Exercise 13.1:

Substitute the following mass quantifiers into the sentences given.

EXAMPLE:

I PLENTY WORK LEFT.   'I have a lot of work left (to do)'.
  (A-LITTLE)
    I A-LITTLE WORK LEFT.   'I have a little work left (to do).'

1. HE CRAZY-FOR CHEESE, HAVE SOME I.   (PLENTY)

    _____ t _____
2. SPORTS THING RESIDENTIAL-SCHOOL HAVE PLENTY.   (SOME)

    ___ t ___
3. WATER CALIFORNIA NOW HAVE A-LITTLE.   (PLENTY)

    _ t ___
4. MEAT IT HAVE LEFT IT SOME.   (A-LITTLE)

    ____ t ___
5. YOUR PIE GRANDMOTHER WANT A-LITTLE.   (SOME)

More on Quantifiers

Some classifiers also serve as quantifiers. The classifiers below are used to indicate:
1. the amount of liquid,
2. the thickness of a solid,
3. the height of a stack.
They are:

CL:G	CL:Ḷ	CL:BB↑↓

133

EXAMPLES:

A. MUST I READ CL:BB↑↓ BOOK FOR CLASS.   'I have to read a big stack of books for class.'

B. STILL LEFT CL:G WINE.   <u>   q   </u> YOU WANT YOU?   'There's still a little wine left. Do you want some?'

134

C. SHE BUY R-U-G NEW. WOW CL:Ḻ. 'She bought a new rug. It's very thick.'

Exercise 13.2:

Substitute the quantifier in the sentence for the one given in parentheses.

EXAMPLE:

CAN SKI, SNOW NOW CL:Ḻ.   'It's possible to ski; the snow is a few inches deep.'
  (CL:BB↑↓)
    CAN SKI, SNOW NOW CL:BB↑↓.   'It's possible to ski; the snow is very deep.'

  _ t __
1. DOG IT WANT CL:G WATER.   (CL:Ḻ)

2. MY HOUSE WOW DIRTY.   HAVE CL:Ḻ D-U-S-T.   (CL:G)

3. BASEMENT, I FIND CL:Ḻ WATER.   (CL:BB↑↓)

4. YESTERDAY, CL:Ḻ PAPER I THROW-AWAY.   (CL:BB↑↓)

5. CL:G O-J YOU DRINK SHOULD YOU.   (CL:Ḻ)

6. RECENTLY HE-GIVE-ME CL:Ḻ LETTER.   (CL:BB↑↓)

7. RAIN STOP FINISH, LEFT M-U-D CL:G.   (CL:Ḻ)

135

More on Plurals

There are two other ways to make plurals of count nouns. (Two ways were discussed earlier in Lesson 7.) They are:

1. Add a classifier which functions as a quantifier, such as CL:5̈, either before the noun or at the end of the sentence.

EXAMPLE:

I SEE CAT CL:55̈.   'I saw a large number of cats.'

I SEE CL:55̈ CAT.   'I saw a large number of cats.'

2. Some nouns can be reduplicated, that is, the sign can be made again several times as it is moved to the side (represented by ++).

EXAMPLE:

IT HOME HAVE TREE + +.   'There are many trees near my home.'

Exercise 13.3:

Change the form of the plural nouns in the sentences below to the plural form given in parentheses.

EXAMPLE:

SHE BRING-THERE 5 SUITCASE.   'She brought 5 suitcases there.'
(Reduplicate)
SHE BRING-THERE SUITCASE ++.   'She brought many suitcases there.'

1. STORE IT HAVE SEVERAL BICYCLE.   (CL:5̈5̈)

2. H-O-T-E-L IT HAVE MANY DOOR.   (Reduplicate)

3. MY SISTER FINISH HAVE 5 BOYFRIEND.   (CL:5̈5̈)

4. I LIKE HOUSE WITH WINDOW MANY.   (Reduplicate)

5. THERE PARTY I SEE A-FEW CHILDREN.   (CL:5̈5̈)

6. I MUST WRITE 4 LIST.   (Reduplicate)

7. HE HAVE MANY BEAUTIFUL GLASS.   (Reduplicate)

More on Using Numbers

1. The sign for 1-CENT or 'penny' is:

1-CENT

Other numbers can be incorporated in this sign to indicate different amounts:

EXAMPLES:

A. I HAVE 25-CENT I. 'I have a quarter.'

B. WE MUST PAY-HIM 30-CENT. 'We have to pay him 30 cents.'

2. The sign for 1-DOLLAR is:

1-DOLLAR

The numbers 1 through 10 can be incorporated in this sign. The numbers 11 and greater do not incorporate; they are followed by a separate sign, DOLLAR.

EXAMPLES:

_t_
A. FOOD COST 5-DOLLAR IT. 'The food cost 5 dollars.'

_____t_____
B. 25 DOLLAR YOU OWE-ME.   'You owe me 25 dollars.'

Exercise 13.4:

Substitute the amount given in parentheses for the amount in the sentences below.

EXAMPLE:

_____q_____
YOU HAVE 10-CENT YOU?   'Do you have a dime?'
   (5-CENT)

   _____q_____
   YOU HAVE 5-CENT YOU?   'Do you have a nickel?'

___t_____
1. BIRTHDAY HE-GIVE-ME 5-DOLLAR.   (7-DOLLAR)

2. I FIND 1-CENT YESTERDAY I.   (50-CENT)

3. I WIN 500 DOLLAR I.   (300 DOLLAR)

4. LONG-AGO T-T-Y COST 60 DOLLAR.   (40 DOLLAR)

5. LONG-AGO I BUY PENCIL COST 2-CENT.   (4-CENT)

   _____t_____
6. MY CAR OLD SELL 150 DOLLAR.   (450 DOLLAR)

   _____q_____
7. 10-DOLLAR YOU NEED TODAY?   (20 DOLLAR)

139

Vocabulary

A-LITTLE

A-LOT, much

ALWAYS

APPOINTMENT, RESERVE, reservation

BASEMENT, below, beneath

BORN, BIRTHDAY, birth

BOYFRIEND

1-CENT, penny

CHEESE

COST, value, worth, price

COUNTRY

140

CRAZY-FOR, favorite

DISCUSS, debate, argue

1-DOLLAR

EMBARRASS

ENOUGH

FREE, safe

FUN

INTELLIGENT, smart

LAW, legal

LIST, outline

NATIONAL, nation

OFTEN, frequently

141

OWE, debt, obligation

PIE

PLENTY

PRICE, cost, charge, tax

REASON, realize, rationale

RIGHT (legal, moral)

RULE

SKI
Noun: SKIING

SNOW

SOME

SOMETIMES, occasionally

STRANGE, odd, peculiar, weird

THROW-AWAY, discard

TROUBLE

WINE

WITH, together

NOTES

DIALOGUE 4

Bill makes arrangements with Jack to see a new play production with Deaf actors.

Bill: KNOW-THAT HAVE PERFORMANCE NEW? DEAF PERFORMANCE

GROUP THERE L-A ESTABLISH.   WANT SEE YOU?

Jack: I WANT.   CHAIR LEFT HAVE?

Bill: SHOULD HAVE LEFT CL:5̈.   I-TTY-IT, TWO-US RESERVE
CHAIR.

TICKET COST 3-DOLLAR.

Jack: I-PAY-YOU NOW CAN I.   WANT TWO-US WITH DRIVE-THERE?

Bill: FINE.   TWO-US WATCH PERFORMANCE FINISH, GO-THERE
FRIEND HOUSE PARTY, CHAT FRIEND FINISH, COME-HERE
HOME.

Jack: TOMORROW I-MEET-YOU TIME?

Bill: TIME 4.   TWO-US TIME PLENTY DRIVE-THERE.

More Negatives

There are other ways to form negative sentences:

1. Use of NEVER. NEVER occurs either before the verb or at the end of the sentence.
   EXAMPLE:

```
_____ n _____
I EXERCISE NEVER I.    'I never exercise.'
```

```
_____ n _____
I NEVER EXERCISE I.    'I never exercise.'
```

2. Use of NONE to mean 'not,' or 'not at all.' Verbs like HAVE, SEE, UNDERSTAND, FEEL, HEAR, EAT, and GET are frequently negated with NONE. NONE may occur either before or after the verb, but when it occurs after the verb, the two signs are often blended together in a single, smooth movement.

   EXAMPLES:

```
_t___ _____ n _____
A.  FRIEND I SEE~ NONE SINCE.    'I haven't seen my friend for a long time.'
```

B. EXPLANATION I UNDERSTAND~NONE I.
   'I didn't understand the explanation.' or 'I didn't understand the explanation at all.'
   _t_ _____n_____
C. T-T-Y I HAVE~ NONE I.   'I don't have a TTY.'

Exercise 14.1:

Change the following sentences to negative sentences with the negative sign given.

EXAMPLE:

I GO-AWAY MOVIE I.   'I go to the movies.'
   (NEVER)
                    _____ n_____
   I NEVER GO-AWAY MOVIE I.   'I never go to the movies.'
                    _____ n_____
   I GO-AWAY MOVIE NEVER I.   'I never go to the movies.'

1. I HEAR YOU MARRY YOU.   (NONE)

   _____ t_____
2. NURSE GIVE-SHOT, I FEEL I.   (NONE)

   ___ t____
3. WRENCH STORE IT HAVE.   (NONE)

4. IT C-O HAVE DEAF WORK.   (NONE)

5. MAN INTERACT DEAF HE.   (NEVER)

   _t_
6. C-F HE GET HE.   (NONE)

   ___t____
7. TURKEY I EAT FINISH.   (NONE)

   _____t_____
8. MONEY YOU-GIVE-HER, I SEE I.   (NONE)

9. SHE-HELP-ME SHE.   (NEVER)

   _t_
10. T-V I UNDERSTAND CAN I.   (NONE)

11. HE BATHE FINISH HE.   (NEVER)

147

Negative Quantifiers

1. NONE may also be used before a noun to show a zero quantity of the noun.

EXAMPLES:

A. I SEE NONE PEOPLE I.   'I saw no people.'

B. I BUY NONE CLOTHES I.   'I bought no clothes.'

2. NOTHING is also used to indicate zero quantity; it is used after the verb.

EXAMPLES:

A. I BUY NOTHING I.   'I bought nothing.'

B. I SEE NOTHING I.   'I saw nothing.'

C. HE FEEL NOTHING HE.   'He felt nothing.'

Exercise 14.2:

Change the following sentences to sentences with the negative quantifiers NONE or NOTHING.

EXAMPLE:

<u>   t   </u>
THERE STORE, I SEE A-FEW PEOPLE.   'I saw a few people at the store.'
  (NONE)
     <u>   t   </u> <u>   n   </u>
    THERE STORE, I SEE NONE PEOPLE.   'I saw no people at the store.'

1. SHE BUY HAMMER AND SCREWDRIVER.   (NOTHING)

2. NOW YEAR, I GROW V-E-G.   (NOTHING)

     <u>   t   </u>
3. NURSE GIVE-SHOT, I FEEL I.   (NOTHING)

4. PEOPLE RIDE B-U-S A-FEW.   (NONE)

   <u> t </u>
5. Z-O-O IT HAVE MONKEY A-FEW.   (NONE)

6. I MUST SHOP, HAVE A-LITTLE FOOD LEFT.   (NONE)

    <u>   t </u>
7. WORK P-O, HE EARN A-LOT.   (NOTHING)

          <u> y </u>
8. REALLY I-INFORM-YOU, HAVE TIME I.   (NONE)

9. YESTERDAY FRIEND HE LEARN SIGN.   (NONE)

   <u> t </u>
10. A-A-A-D, I DO-WORK.   (NOTHING)

Use of NOTHING

In sentences like the following, NOTHING has the meaning of a denial of a preceding accusation. The accusation usually has a topic marker.

EXAMPLES:

___ t ____ ____ n ___
A. I HIT BOY, NOTHING I!   'I didn't hit the boy!'

_____ q _____
B. **Question:** GLASS SHE BREAK?   'Did she break the glass?'
_____ n _____
Response: NOTHING SHE.   'No, she didn't.'

Exercise 14.3:

Add NOTHING to the following sentences:

EXAMPLE:

I LOSE YOUR KEY.   'I lost your keys.'
_____ t _____ ____ n ___
I LOSE YOUR KEY, NOTHING I!   'I didn't lose your keys!'

__ t ___
1. LETTER SHE-SEND-HIM.

2. SHIRT NEW WASH-IN-MACHINE.

3. I RESPONSIBLE CAR-ACCIDENT I.

4. I I-TTY-YOU YESTERDAY NIGHT.

5. I I-WARN-HIM FINISH.

6. I-BOTHER-HIM I.

7. BOY STEAL CAMERA HE.

Vocabulary

ANYWAY, regardless, it doesn't matter

BATHE
Noun: bath

BOTHER, disturb

CAR-ACCIDENT, collide, collision

CHASE

CONFUSED, mixed up

CURIOUS

DO-WORK, labor

EARN

EXERCISE, work out

FALSE, fake

FREEZE, frozen

GIVE-SHOT

HAMMER

HIT

INTERACT, associate, socialize

LAZY

MONKEY

NERVOUS

NEVER

NONE

NOTHING

NURSE

PATIENT, patience, endure, bear

PLAY

PUZZLED, perplexed

QUICK, fast, rapid

REAL, true

REALLY, TRUE, sure

REQUIRE, demand

RIDE
Noun: ride,
transportation

SCIENCE

SCREWDRIVER

SHAVE
Noun: shaver, razor

SHOP, shopping

SHOWER

SINCE, lately

SPEND, pay

TAKE-PICTURE
Noun: camera

TURKEY

WARN, caution

WRENCH

NOTES

LESSON 15

More Directional Verbs

Some directional verbs such as CHOOSE, COPY, TAKE, SUMMON, TAKE-ADVANTAGE-OF and BORROW have a movement opposite of other directional verbs such as GIVE, TELL, SHOW, ASK, INFORM.

I-CHOOSE-YOU	I-GIVE-YOU

I-SUMMON-YOU	I-INFORM-YOU

The other forms of CHOOSE and similar directional verbs are:

YOU-CHOOSE-ME	SHE-CHOOSE-ME

SHE-CHOOSE-HIM	I-CHOOSE-HER

SHE-CHOOSE-YOU	YOU-CHOOSE-HER

Exercise 15.1:

Change the following I to you verb forms to I to he/she/it verb forms.

EXAMPLE:

<pre>
                    q
YOUR PAPER I-COPY-YOU CAN I?   'Can I copy from your paper?'
                  q
  HER PAPER I-COPY-HER CAN I?   'Can I copy from her paper?'
</pre>

<pre>
                        q
1. DON'T-MIND I-BORROW-YOU DICTIONARY?
                      n
2. I UNDERSTAND.   I DON'T-WANT I-TAKE-ADVANTAGE-YOU.
   _t__
3. READY, I HAPPY I-SUMMON-YOU.
        t
4. YOUR SCHEDULE I-COPY-YOU CAN I.

5. I WANT I-CHOOSE-YOU.
</pre>

Exercise 15.2:

Change the following <u>you to me</u> verb forms to <u>you to he/she/it</u> verb forms.

EXAMPLE:

YOU-TELL-ME FINISH YOU-CHOOSE-ME FOR COMMITTEE.
'You already told me that you picked me for the committee.'
  YOU-TELL-ME FINISH YOU-CHOOSE-HIM FOR COMMITTEE.
  'You already told me that you picked him for the committee.'

      _____ t _____
1. MY HOMEWORK YOU-COPY-ME.
              _____ q _____
2. CAN YOU-TAKE-ME THERE Z-O-O?
      _____ t _____
3. YOU READY LEAVE, YOU-SUMMON-ME.
        _____n_____
4. NOT LIKE YOU-TAKE-ADVANTAGE-ME.

5. SURPRISE YOU-CHOOSE-ME PRESIDENT C-L-U-B.

Directional Verbs Incorporating Two Objects

Directional verbs can change their movement to show the number of persons or objects. The inflection for two objects, YOU-TWO or TWO-THEM has the following form:

I-INFORM-YOU-TWO	I-INFORM-TWO-THEM

Exercise 15.3:

Change the following singular object verb forms to dual (two) objects.

EXAMPLE:

HAPPY I I-INFORM-YOU HAPPEN.   'I can let you know what happened.'
  HAPPY I I-INFORM-YOU-TWO HAPPEN.   'I can let the two of you know what happened.'

1. YESTERDAY I I-TELL-HIM, RAIN WILL.
     __ t __
2. MONEY HE-GIVE-HER.

3. BETTER YOU-ASK-HIM. SURE YOU RIGHT YOU.

4. I WANT I-TAKE-YOU THERE RESTAURANT.

5. YOU BEST, I WANT I-CHOOSE-YOU.

6. BEER I-CL:C-GIVE-HER.

     ___ t ____
7. DAUGHTER I I-SEND-HER LETTER WILL I.

Directional Verbs Incorporating EACH or ALL

Directional verbs also change to indicate 'to each of you/them,' or 'to all of you/them.'
The forms of these inflections are:

I-TELL-EACH-OF-YOU	I-TELL-EACH-OF-THEM

I-TELL-ALL-OF-YOU

I-TELL-ALL-OF-THEM

Exercise 15.4:

Change the following singular object verb forms to plural forms using either EACH or ALL as indicated.

EXAMPLE:

  __ t ____

TROPHY HE-PRESENT-HER.　'He gave her a trophy.'
  (EACH)
    __ t ___

    TROPHY HE-PRESENT-EACH-OF-THEM.　'He gave a trophy to each of them.'

  __ t __

1. THIEF COP FINISH HE-CATCH-HER.　(EACH)

          _____ q _____

2. PLEASE FOR ME, CAN YOU YOU-ASK-HIM?　(ALL)

3. WANT I I-INVITE-HER MY WEDDING.　(EACH)

4. TOMORROW I I-INFORM-YOU WHO WIN.　(ALL)

    _____ t _____

5. MY OLD CLOTHES WILL I I-GIVE-TWO-THEM.　(ALL)

6. FINISH I I-TELL-YOU MUST YOU COME-HERE TIME 8.　(ALL)

          _____ t _____

7. TWO-OF-THEM CHILDREN MOTHER SHE-SEND-TWO-THEM BOX.　(EACH)

Vocabulary

ALONE

BEER

BEST

BETTER

BORROW

CAREFUL, be careful

CARELESS

CHOOSE, pick

COMMITTEE

COPY, imitate

DICTIONARY

DON'T-MIND, don't care

DRY, boring

EXAGGERATE

FINALLY, succeed

GOVERNMENT, capitol

HAPPEN, occur, incident

HIRE, INVITE, welcome

IMPOSSIBLE

JEALOUS, envious

JOIN, participate

KILL, murder

LISTEN

LOAN, lend

MEMBER

OFFER, propose, suggest

POLITE, manners

PRESENT, give

READY

SAME-TIME,
simultaneously

SCHEDULE

SUCCEED, success

SUMMON, call

TAKE, take out

TAKE-ADVANTAGE-OF,
rip off

163

THIEF

THIN

TROPHY

WORSE

NOTES

Time Measurements Incorporating Number

The time signs MINUTE, HOUR, DAY, WEEK, and MONTH (but not YEAR) incorporate the numbers 1-9:

5-HOUR	3-DAY
8-WEEK	9-MONTH

MINUTE can incorporate the numbers 1-10:

2-MINUTE

but,

4-YEAR

166

Exercise 16.1:

Substitute the amount given in parentheses for the amount in the sentences below.

EXAMPLE:

I I-MEET-YOU 2-MINUTE I.   'I'll meet you in 2 minutes.'
   (5-MINUTE)
      I I-MEET-YOU 5-MINUTE I.   'I'll meet you in 5 minutes.'

1. MOVIE IT CONTINUE 2-HOUR.   (3-HOUR)

   __ t __
2. COURSE I TAKE-UP 6-WEEK.   (8-WEEK)

3. NOW TWO-US MARRY 4 YEAR.   (7 YEAR)

4. FIVE-US PLAN GO-AWAY BACKPACKING MAYBE 4-DAY.   (5-DAY)

5. NOW LEFT 3-MONTH, MOVE-AWAY WILL I.   (6-MONTH)

6. I ORDER BED NEW, I MUST WAIT 8-WEEK.   (4-WEEK)

7. HE LOSE ALMOST 8-DAY.   (9-DAY)

Tense Indicators Incorporating Number

The tense indicators NEXT-WEEK, LAST-WEEK, NEXT-MONTH, NEXT-YEAR, and LAST-YEAR can also incorporate some numbers. But they vary in which numbers they can incorporate.

NEXT-WEEK incorporates
the numbers 1-9.

LAST-WEEK incorporates
the numbers 1-9.

IN-FOUR-WEEK

FIVE-WEEK-AGO

NEXT-MONTH incorporates
the numbers 1-9.

NEXT-YEAR incorporates
the numbers 1-5.

IN-SIX-MONTH

IN-THREE-YEAR

LAST-YEAR incorporates
the numbers 1-5.

TWO-YEAR-AGO

Exercise 16.2:

Substitute the tense indicator given in parentheses for the tense indicator in the sentences.

EXAMPLE:

_____ q _____
NEXT-WEEK SISTER COME-HERE? 'Is your sister coming next week?'
(IN-TWO-WEEK)

_____ q _____
IN-TWO-WEEK SISTER COME-HERE? 'Is your sister coming in 2 weeks?'

1. F-R-A-T MEETING WILL HERE IN-TWO-YEAR. (IN-FOUR-YEAR)

__q__
2. LAST TIME I I-SEE-YOU 3-YEAR-AGO, RIGHT? (LAST-YEAR)

168

3. 20 YEAR PAST HARD FIND INTERPRETER. (25 YEAR)

4. PARTY THERE MY HOME IN-TWO-MONTH. (IN-THREE-MONTH)

5. I GO-THERE FINISH FOUR-WEEK-AGO. (SIX-WEEK-AGO)

6. HE GRADUATE GALLAUDET 5-YEAR-AGO. (FOUR-YEAR-AGO)

7. C-O SAY WILL BRING-HERE BED IN-SIX-WEEK. (IN-FOUR-WEEK)

Time Reduplication

The signs HOUR, WEEK, MONTH, and NEXT-YEAR can be reduplicated to mean 'hourly,' 'weekly,' 'monthly,' and 'yearly.'

EXAMPLE:

I MUST GO-THERE DOCTOR WEEKLY. 'I must go to the doctor every week.'

HOURLY	WEEKLY	MONTHLY

However, 'daily' has the following form:

YEARLY	DAILY

Exercise 16.3:

Substitute the reduplicated signs in parentheses for those given in the sentences.

EXAMPLE:

__t___
FRIEND I SHOULD GO-THERE VISIT DAILY.   'I should go to visit my friend every
                                                          day.'

    (WEEKLY)
     ___t__
    FRIEND I SHOULD GO-THERE VISIT WEEKLY.   'I should go to visit my friend
    every week.'

1. IT-SEND-ME NEWSPAPER WEEKLY.   (MONTHLY)

2. MUST I TAKE-PILL HOURLY.   (DAILY)

3. SHE GO-THERE EUROPE BUSINESS YEARLY.   (MONTHLY)

4. SHE EXERCISE DAILY.   (WEEKLY)

5. HE TO-TELEPHONE I WEEKLY, I BORED I.   (DAILY)

NOTE: More on Time Repetition

Some forms of time that occur regularly are not repeated but use a single movement.
1. To show EVERY-MONDAY, -TUESDAY, -WEDNESDAY, etc., a downward movement is used:

EVERY-SUNDAY

EVERY-SATURDAY

2. To show EVERY-MORNING, -AFTERNOON, -NOON, -NIGHT, a sideward movement is used:

EVERY-MORNING

EVERY-NOON

Vocabulary

ANIMAL

BACKPACKING

BIRD, chicken

BORED

BOSS

BUSY, business

CITY, town, community

COMPLAIN, complaint, gripe

CONTINUE, last

COW

DAILY, usual, ordinary

DIFFICULT, difficulty

EUROPE

EXPERIENCE

FISH

GALLAUDET

GIVE-UP, surrender

GRADUATE

HURRY, rush

INCREASE, raise, add

INTERPRET

INTERRUPT

LAST, final, end

MOUSE

MOVE-AWAY

PAST

PIG, pork

PITY, sympathy

PLEASANT, friendly

PRINT, publish
Noun: NEWSPAPER

SOPHISTICATED, prim

START, begin

TAKE-PILL
Noun: pill

TOTAL, add, add up

DIALOGUE 5

A group of Deaf people are meeting at Bill's home to watch a captioned film.

_____

          _____ n _____   _ q _

Jane: YOU, I SEE~NONE SINCE. I HEAR YOU NEW WORK. FINE?

                     _____ t _____ ___ n ___

Ron: FINE. ALONE DEAF. THEY KNOW SIGN NOTHING. I DECIDE
ESTABLISH SIGN CLASS. 2-HOUR EVERY-TUESDAY AND
EVERY-THURSDAY. WOW IMPROVE.

                       _____ q _____

Jane: GOOD IDEA YOU. YOUR BOSS SIGN, FINGERSPELL?

Ron: A-LITTLE. I HAVE 3 BOSS. I PRESENT-EACH SIGN
BOOK. THEY LEARN A-LITTLE. NEXT-WEEK I GET T-T-Y
SHOULD. YOU-TTY-ME CAN YOU.

Jane: WOW FINE. TWO-WEEK-AGO MY GROUP INCREASE 1 DEAF,

                                         _____ q ____

NOW HAVE TOTAL 6 DEAF WORK MY C-O. YOUR C-O HIRE

_____

DEAF MORE WILL?

        __ y ___

Ron: SHOULD.

        __ q ___

Bill: READY? NOW MOVIE START.

175

LESSON 17

Using a Clause as Topic

1. Some verbs such as WANT, DON'T-WANT, KNOW, DON'T-KNOW, LIKE, DON'T-LIKE, KNOW-THAT, FEEL, DECIDE, HOPE, SEE, DOUBT, TEND can be preceded by a topicalized clause.

EXAMPLES:

```
           _____t_____   _____n_____
A.  GO-AWAY TOMORROW, I DON'T-WANT I.   'I don't want to leave tomorrow.'
```

```
           _____t_____   _____y_____
B.  HE LIKE SHE GIRL, I KNOW-THAT I.   'I know that he likes the girl.'
           _____t_____   ____n_____
C.  TWO-US LEAVE TIME 7 MORNING, SHE DOUBT.   'She doubts that we will
    leave at 7 A.M.'
```

2. Also, the negatives NOT, NEVER, NONE and NOTHING can be preceded by a topicalized clause.

EXAMPLES:

```
           _____t_____   __n_
A.  GO-AWAY TOMORROW, NOT I.   'I'm not leaving tomorrow.'
     ____t____   __n__
B.  I EXERCISE, NEVER.   'I never exercise.'
```

Exercise 17.1:

Change the following sentences to sentences with topicalized clauses.

EXAMPLE:

<u>   y   </u>
I KNOW-THAT HE AGAIN LATE. 'I know he'll be late again.'

<u>   t   </u> <u>   y   </u>
HE AGAIN LATE, I KNOW-THAT. 'I know he'll be late again.'

<u>   n   </u>
1. I DON'T-KNOW FINISH ADVERTISE TOURNAMENT.

<u>   n   </u>
2. HE DOUBT HE APPLY FOR PRESIDENT.

3. TWO-THEM TEND ARGUE ALL-DAY.

4. HE KNOW-THAT I SUPPORT WHEELCHAIR.

<u>   n   </u>
5. SHE DON'T-WANT BORROW MONEY FROM BOSS.

<u>   n   </u>
6. I DON'T-WANT I AGAIN BROKE.

7. THREE-US WANT GO-BY-BOAT THERE EUROPE.

<u>   n   </u>
8. HE NOT FIRED.

9. GRANDFATHER LIKE TELL-STORY.

<u>   n   </u>
10. I DON'T-LIKE STAY PARTY ALL-NIGHT.

Comparative Sentences

When comparing two persons, places, things or ideas, the following procedure is used.
1. First establish one person, place, thing or idea on one side of the body and the other on the other side.
2. Then indicate which one you will comment upon.

EXAMPLES:

_____ t _____
A. WASHINGTON, NEW-YORK, I PREFER IT. (Washington).
   'I prefer Washington to New York.'

_____ t _____
B. CAR IT HAVE RADIO, A-C; IT PLAIN, I WANT IT. (the plain one).
   'I want the plain car rather than the one with a radio and air conditioner.'

3. A person, place, thing or idea can be established in a pronoun location to show a relationship with that pronoun.

_____ t _____
C. MY SISTER, YOUR SISTER, SHE (my sister) OLDER SHE.
   'My sister is older than yours.'

178

Exercise 17.2:

Combine the following sentences to form comparative sentences.

EXAMPLE:

HE COOK HE.   HE WASH-DISH HE.   'He cooks. He washes dishes.'
  (PREFER)
        ____ t ____
    COOK, WASH-DISH, HE PREFER IT.   'He prefers to cook rather than to wash
                                    dishes.'

1. HOUSE R-E-N-T, A-P-T R-E-N-T.   (WORSE)

2. IT WOOD TABLE, IT METAL TABLE.   (WANT)

3. STAY HOME WATCH T-V, GO-AWAY MOVIE PAY 5-DOLLAR.   (BETTER)

4. IT FLOWER REAL, IT FLOWER S-I-L-K.   (PRETTIER)

                              ____ q ____
5. IT EXPENSIVE, IT CHEAP.   (YOU WANT?)

6. I GO-THERE COLLEGE, I STAY WORK.   (STAY)

7. MEETING HERE, MEETING THERE.   (PREFER)

Conjunctions

The signs WRONG, HAPPEN, HIT, FRUSTRATE, and FIND can be used as conjunctions. Some of their meanings as conjunctions are:

WRONG   'without warning, suddenly'
FRUSTRATE   'to be prevented from'
HIT   'unexpectedly, turned out that'
FIND   'find out that'
HAPPEN   'happened that'

EXAMPLES:

A. I WALK, WRONG RAIN. 'As I was walking, it suddenly started raining.'

_____ n_____

B. I PLAN PARTY, FIND HE CAN'T COME-HERE.
   'I was planning the party, then I found out that he couldn't come.'
C. HE GO-AWAY VACATION 1-WEEK, HIT LAID-UP SICK.
   'He went on vacation for a week and unexpectedly became ill.'
D. I CHAT HAPPEN HE-TELL-ME HE FROM WASHINGTON.
   'I was talking with him and he happened to tell me he was from Washington.'
E. TONIGHT TWO-US WANT SEE MOVIE, FRUSTRATE CLOSE.
   'We wanted to see the movie tonight but it was closed.'

Exercise 17.3:

Combine the sentences below, using the conjunction given.

EXAMPLE:

TWO-THEM STEADY-DATE 6-MONTH.   'They were dating for 6 months'.
TWO-THEM MARRY.   'They got married.'
   (WRONG)
      TWO-THEM STEADY-DATE 6-MONTH, WRONG MARRY.
      'They were dating for 6 months, and before you knew it they got married.'

1. SHE RESEARCH A-S-L.
   SHE FIND RULE + +.   (HIT)

2. SHE GO-THERE BUY T-T-Y.
   T-T-Y S-A-L-E.   (HAPPEN)

3. BABY SEEM SICK.
   BABY HAVE EAR-ACHE.   (FIND)

4. CLOTHES PUT-IN WASH-IN-MACHINE.
   CLOTHES RUIN.   (FRUSTRATE)

5. I BUY GLASS NEW.
   GLASS DAMAGE.   (WRONG)

6. TWO-US CHAT.
   TWO-US SAME HAVE DEAF PARENTS.   (FIND)

7. I WATCH T-V.
   T-V CAPTION.   (WRONG)

8. I DRIVE-THERE.
   SHE NOT HOME.   (FRUSTRATE)

9. HE HAVE NEW CAR.
   CAR STEAL.   (FRUSTRATE)

10. HE ACT NOTHING-TO-IT.
    HE SHOT-UP FAMOUS.   (WRONG)

Vocabulary

APPLY, volunteer, candidate

ARGUE, quarrel

BROKE

BUT

CAPTION, sub-titles

COMPARE
Noun: comparison

DAMAGE, destroy

DOUBT

EARACHE

EAST

FAMOUS

FIRE (from job)

FRUSTRATE

FRUSTRATE (conjunction)

HIT (conjunction)

HOPE, EXPECT

LAID-UP

LATE

LIE-DOWN

METAL

NAB, get ahold of

NORTH

NOTHING-TO-IT

PUT-IN

RADIO

RENT

RESEARCH

RETIRE, loaf
Noun: VACATION

RUBBER

RUIN, spoiled

183

SEEM, appears

 SHOT-UP, become successful

 SOMETHING, someone, alone

 SOUTH

 STEADY-DATE

 SUPPORT, sponsor, advocate

 TEND

 TOURNAMENT

 WEST

 WHEELCHAIR

 WOOD

 WRONG (conjunction)

184

NOTES

LESSON 18

Verb Inflection: -REPEATEDLY

Many action verbs can be repeated to show a repeated or regular action. Frequently the following facial adverbs are used with verbs inflected for -REPEATEDLY.

'with effort or difficulty'

'with ease, pleasure'	'with attention, care, deliberately'	'without attention, carelessly, foolishly'

EXAMPLE:

```
_____t_____
```
A. DEAF GROUP I LIKE GO-THERE-REPEATEDLY CHAT.
   'I like to go often to talk with deaf people.'

B. DAILY I-TELL-HER-REPEATEDLY, SHE NOT UNDERSTAND.
   'I've told her every day, but she still doesn't understand.'
                                        _____ n _____
C. SINCE LETTER I I-SEND-HIM-REPEATEDLY, HEAR~ NONE I.
   'I kept sending him letters, but I heard nothing from him.'

Exercise 18.1:

Change the following underlined verb forms to the -REPEATEDLY form, and use the facial adverb given in parentheses.

EXAMPLE:

TWO-THEM CHILDREN FIGHT.   'The two children got into a fight.'
   (with effort)
      TWO-THEM CHILDREN FIGHT-REPEATEDLY.   'The two children fight all the
                                                                    time.'

1. YESTERDAY NIGHT I-TTY-YOU, YOU NONE YOU.   (with effort)

   _____ t _____
2. PITY-HIM, TEAM HIS LOUSY, HE LOSE-COMPETITION.   (carelessly)

3. BROTHER TEND ANALYZE MOVIE.   (with attention)

4. SHE BOTHER-HIM, WRONG HE-BAWL-OUT-HER.   (carelessly)

   ___ t ___
5. HE THIRSTY.   WATER HE DRINK.   (with effort)

6. SHE LOVE READ.   (with ease)

   _____ t _____
7. BASKETBALL, NEW-YORK BEFORE WIN.   (with ease)

8. FINISH I-WARN-YOU SHOULD FIX T-I-R-E.   (with effort)

9. BORED I I-PRESENT-YOU MONEY.   (with effort)

10. FIND HE INFORM-HIM POLICE.   (with attention)

Verb Inflection: -CONTINUALLY

Many verbs inflect by adding a circular movement to show a continuing action. Facial adverbs used with -REPEATEDLY can also be used with the -CONTINUALLY inflection.

EXAMPLES:

A. B-U-S NOT COME, I STAND-CONTINUALLY.
   'I stood around waiting for the bus. It didn't come.'

B. ALL-DAY I WORK-CONTINUALLY, NOT EXPECT TIME 6 I.
   'I worked without stopping all day and didn't realize it was 6 o'clock.'

Exercise 18.2:

Change the underlined verb forms to the -CONTINUALLY form, and use the facial adverb given in parentheses.

EXAMPLE:

<u>   t </u>
DENTIST, I <u>WAIT</u>.   'I sat waiting for the dentist.'
  (with effort)
    <u> t </u>
    DENTIST, I WAIT-CONTINUALLY.   'I sat for a long while waiting for the dentist.'

1. HE <u>STAY-THERE</u> 3-HOUR FINISH COME-HERE. (with ease)

2. HE APPEAR NONE, I <u>WAIT</u>. (with effort)

3. TRAVEL, I <u>WANT</u>. (with effort)

4. SHE <u>EAT</u>, WRONG BECOME-FAT.   (carelessly)

5. HARD UNDERSTAND HE <u>FINGERSPELL</u>.   (with attention)

6. WOOD <u>BURN</u> 3-HOUR.   (with ease)

7. HOMEWORK I <u>STRUGGLE</u>, FINALLY UNDERSTAND I.   (with effort)

Vocabulary

ANALYZE, research

BECOME-FAT

BRIGHT, CLEAR, obvious

BUTTER

CELEBRATE, anniversary

COMFORTABLE

CONFIDENT, confidence

DARK

DENTIST

EGG

ELECTRIC, electricity

EMPHASIZE, impress, stress

EXACT, perfect, precise

FIGHT

FIX

HIDE

IMPRESSED

JUMP

KNEEL

LICENSE

LONG (time)

LOSE-COMPETITION

LOUSY

MIRROR

MUSIC, song

PEPPER

POISON

POTATO

PULL

PUSH

SALT

SELFISH, greedy

SOUR, bitter

191

STAND STRUGGLE TEAM

TRAVEL, tour VERY

NOTES

LESSON 19

Adjective Modulation: VERY-

Adjectives can change their movement to add an adverbial meaning. The movement added to adjectives to mean 'very' has the following form:
1. The beginning of the sign has a hold which appears "tense,"
2. Then there is a quick release.
Note the facial adverb commonly used with the VERY-modulation shown below.

MAD	VERY-MAD

FAST	VERY-FAST

SLOW	VERY-SLOW

Exercise 19.1:

Change the adjectives in the following sentences by adding the modulation VERY-.

EXAMPLE:

BUILDING IT OLD.   'The building is old.'
 BUILDING IT VERY-OLD.   'The building is very old.'

1. K-A-N-S-A-S CL:BB.

2. WINTER THERE M-I-N-N COLD.

3. HER HOME WOW SMALL.

4. SNOW ALL-OVER WOW WHITE.

5. YOUR LECTURE CLEAR.

   _____ n _____
6. YOU WORK NOTHING, LAZY YOU.

7. BASKETBALL PLAYER HE WOW TALL.

8. GAS NOW EXPENSIVE.

9. MUST YOU GO-THERE MEETING, IT IMPORTANT.

    ____ t ____
10. RAIN SINCE, WOW WORSE.

Adjective Modulation: -REPEATEDLY

Some adjectives can be repeated to show the meaning of 'repeatedly.' This movement is added to adjectives which describe a temporary condition—in other words, a condition which can start, stop, and then start again.
  Examples of these adjectives are:

ANGRY	MAD	FRUSTRATED	WRONG
SICK	EMBARRASSED	GUILTY	CARELESS
AFRAID	WORRY	NOISE	
HURT	LATE	DIFFERENT	

MAD	MAD-REPEATEDLY

WRONG	WRONG-REPEATEDLY

Exercise 19.2:

Change the underlined adjectives in the following sentences by adding the modulation -REPEATEDLY.

EXAMPLE:

I-TELL-HIM-REPEATEDLY.   HE CARELESS.
  'I have told him many times. He's careless.'
   I-TELL-HIM-REPEATEDLY.   HE CARELESS-REPEATEDLY.
    I have told him many times. He still gets careless.'

                _ whq _
1. SHE MAD.   WRONG?

2. FOOTBALL PLAYER HE HURT.

3. FATHER WORRY.   I LATE I.

          _____ n _____
4. SINCE DON'T-KNOW WHY, I SICK.

5. DOWNSTAIRS HAVE DOG, NOISE AWFUL.

196

6. HE JUDGMENT NONE, HE <u>WRONG</u>.

7. HE LOOK-FOR WORK, <u>FRUSTRATE</u> HE.

Adjective Modulation:-CONTINUALLY

Adjectives which describe a temporary condition can also be inflected to show the meaning of 'continually.' This inflection is made by adding a circular movement. Examples of these adjectives are:

CAREFUL	HURT	SILLY	MAD
WRONG	DIFFERENT	EMBARRASSED	FRUSTRATED
AFRAID	SICK	MISCHIEVOUS	

CAREFUL

CAREFUL-CONTINUALLY

HURT

HURT-CONTINUALLY

Exercise 19.3:

Change the underlined adjectives in the following sentences by adding the modulation -CONTINUALLY.

EXAMPLE:

AWFUL HE FALL, BREAK L-E-G.   SINCE <u>HURT</u>.
  'It's terrible! He fell and broke his leg. Since then it has hurt.'
AWFUL HE FALL, BREAK L-E-G.   SINCE HURT-CONTINUALLY.
    'It's terrible! He fell and broke his leg. Since then it has hurt all the time.'

1. LIKE I OUTSIDE SIT, LOOK-AT PEOPLE <u>DIFFERENT</u>.

    _____ t _____
2. PARTY THERE, SHE <u>EMBARRASSED</u> ALL-NIGHT.

    _____ n _____
3. I DON'T-KNOW, SEEM I <u>WRONG</u>.

4. HE BUY NEW CAR, SINCE <u>CAREFUL</u> HE.

5. AUNT <u>SICK</u>.   WRONG LOST #JOB.

6. ALL-DAY GIRL <u>MISCHIEVOUS</u>.

    _____ t _____
7. CAPTION T-V HAVE <u>DIFFERENT-REPEATEDLY</u>.

Vocabulary

ACTION, activities

AFRAID

APPREHENSIVE, guilty

BACK

BLOOD

CAUSE

DANGER, dangerous,
threat

DISMISS, lay off, pardon,
excuse

DOWNSTAIRS

EACH, every

EITHER

FRONT

GOAL, aim, objective

GUESS, assume,
estimate

HABIT, custom, used to

HISTORY

IMAGINE

INCLUDE, involve, everything

#JOB

JUDGE, court

LAND

LOOK-FOR, search, hunt

MISCHIEVOUS

OCEAN

OUTDOORS, outside

200

PRAISE, commend, applaud

PREVENT, block

PROVE, proof

RIVER

ROUGH

RUN-OUT-OF, deplete

SILLY, ridiculous

SUPPOSE, imagine, if

SUPPRESS, restrain

SWALLOW

TEMPERATURE

TOUGH

201

TURN-DOWN, reject   UPSTAIRS   WEIGH, weight, pound

DIALOGUE 6

Don is reminiscing about the "old days".

Don:
<u>   t   n   </u>
LONG-AGO NONE HAVE T-T-Y, T-V CAPTION, INTERPRETER

<u>   </u>
SAME NOW.   YOU-PL. YOUNG HAVE PLENTY.

Mary:
<u>   t   whq   </u>
FIRST T-T-Y YOU BUY WHEN?

Don: LONG-AGO 1971.

Mary:
<u>   whq   </u>
HOW-MUCH COST?

Don:
<u>   t   </u>
60 DOLLAR.   T-T-Y LONG-AGO VERY-BIG, NOW VERY-SMALL,

COST 600 DOLLAR.

Mary: WOW.   IMPORTANT HAVE T-T-Y.

Don: TRUE.   I REMEMBER I WANT GO-THERE VISIT FRIEND, MUST I

DRIVE-THERE.   SOMETIMES I DRIVE-THERE, FRUSTRATE

FRIEND NOT THERE.   MUST GO-THERE-REPEATEDLY FINALLY

NAB FRIEND.   MANY TIME I FRUSTRATE-REPEATEDLY.

Mary: NOW I-TTY-HIM FRIEND, FIND HE NOT HOME.   I SAVE GAS.

Don:
<u>   t   </u>
TRUE.   COMPARE LONG-AGO, NOW IT(now) BETTER.

LESSON 20

Conditional Sentences

Conditional sentences have two parts: *the condition* and *the consequence*. The sentences are made by:

1. Raising the eyebrows during the *condition* (represented by _____ if _____), and lowering them during the *consequence*.
2. Optionally the *condition* may be preceded by either SUPPOSE or #IF.

EXAMPLES:

_____ if _____
A. TOMORROW SNOW, I GO-AWAY SKIING.   'If it snows tomorrow, I'll go skiing.'

_____ if _____
B. SUPPOSE THERE HAVE INTERPRETER, I GO-THERE I.
'If there is an interpreter, I'll go.'
_____ if _____
C. #IF I HEAR~NONE, I PROCEED WILL I.
'If I don't hear anything, I'll go ahead.'

Exercise 20.1:

Combine the following sentences into conditional sentences, using the first sentence as the "condition" and the second as the "consequence."

EXAMPLE:

BOOK NOT ARRIVE.   'The books haven't arrived.'
I PROCEED CLASS.   'I'll go ahead with my class.'
          _____if_____
BOOKS NOT ARRIVE, I PROCEED CLASS.
'If the books haven't arrived, I'll go ahead with my class.'

1. AIRPLANE AGAIN POSTPONE.
   I MAD I.

2. MONEY YOU-GIVE-ME NOW.
   I BUY TICKET I.

   _ t _
3. C-F I GET FINISH.
   I-INFORM-ALL-OF-YOU.

4. YOU DRIVE-THERE.
   I GO-WITH WANT I.

5. T-V CAPTION HAVE HE.
   I GO-THERE HIS HOME.

6. T-V HAVE ACTOR DEAF IT.
   I WATCH MUST I.

7. LEARN SIGN HE WANT.
   PRACTICE MUST HE.

Rhetorical Questions

WH-question signs can be used as rhetorical questions to draw attention to additional information which the signer will provide. However, rhetorical questions differ from ordinary WH-questions in that the eyebrows are raised instead of squeezed together. _____rq _____ indicates raised eyebrows for the rhetorical question.

EXAMPLES:

```
         ___t _____ _n_  _rq_  _____n_____
A.  I BUY T-V CAPTION CAN'T.   WHY?   NONE MONEY I.
    'I can't buy a TV decoder because I don't have any money.'
```

```
                                              _rq_      _____n_____
B.  WILL INFORM-ALL-OF-YOU ABOUT MEETING. WHEN?   DON'T-KNOW I.
    'I don't know when I will inform you of the meeting.'
                             _rq_
C.  SISTER GO-THERE COLLEGE. WHERE?   GALLAUDET.
    'My sister is going to Gallaudet College.'
```

Exercise 20.2:

Add the information in the second sentence to the first sentence, using the WH-question sign given.

EXAMPLE:

```
I GO-AWAY WASHINGTON.   'I'm going to Washington.'
   (HOW)
      I GO-BY-TRAIN   'I'm going by train.'
                      _rq_
      I GO-AWAY WASHINGTON. HOW?   GO-BY-TRAIN.
      'I'm going to Washington by train.'
```

1. THEY FINISH VOTE PRESIDENT C-L-U-B.   (WHO)
   BROTHER PRESIDENT C-L-U-B HE.

2. NOW RESEARCH-REPEATEDLY SIGN.   (WHAT-FOR)
   UNDERSTAND LANGUAGE.

   _t _
3. CAR I FINISH DECIDE BUY.   (WHICH)
   D-A-T-S-U-N I BUY.

4. HE LECTURE-REPEATEDLY.   (WHAT)
   HE LECTURE ABOUT C-L-E-R-C, HIMSELF DEAF.

5. I GO-THERE PUT-IN-GAS.   (HOW-MUCH)
   GAS COST 20 DOLLAR.

6. YOU GO-TO-IT CLOSE-DOOR.   (WHY)
   BUG ENTER-REPEATEDLY.

Vocabulary

ADD-TO, additional

ADMIT, confess

ADULT

AUDIENCE

BECAUSE, since

BRAVE

BUG, insect

CHANGE, alter, modify

CLOSE-DOOR

CONTROL, manage,
direct

COUNT

DENY

DIVIDE, split

EQUAL, even, fair

EXCHANGE, switch,
trade in

FOLLOW

FORBID, illegal, prohibit

HONEST, truth   HONOR   #IF

KEEP, be careful   LESS, reduce   LET, allow, permit

LIMIT, restrict   MEAN, cruel   MEASURE

MULTIPLY

OPPOSE, sue, against
Noun: discrimination,
prejudice

OPPOSITE, counter

POSTPONE, put off

PRISON

PROCEED, get along, go
ahead

PUNISH, penalty

REJECT

RELATIVES

REMOVE, discard

SEPARATE, apart

SHAME

SUBTRACT

VOTE, elect

WASTE

LESSON 21

Pluralizing Classifiers

Pronominal classifiers can be reduplicated to form plurals. Two ways are shown below.

EXAMPLES:

A. WOW BICYCLE CL:3-IN-A-ROW. 'Wow, there are a lot of bicycles lined up in a row.'

B. WOW BICYCLE CL:3-ALL-OVER. 'Wow, there are bicycles all over the place.'

Some other pronominal classifiers are:

CL:Å	CL: ⊢	CL:V̈
For any stationary object such as a house, a vase, a statue, a lamp, a company, a business.	For winged aircraft.	For any small or crouched animal or human such as a frog, a mouse, a child sitting down, or a horse lying down.

C. BEFORE NOTHING, NOW HOUSE CL:Å-ALL-OVER.
 'Before there was nothing, now there are houses all over the place.'

Exercise 21.1:

Change the plural form in the sentences below to the plural form given in parentheses by using a classifier.

EXAMPLE:

I WALK, SEE RABBIT MANY.   'I was walking and saw many rabbits.'
 (ALL-OVER)
  I WALK, SEE RABBIT CL:V̈-ALL-OVER.   'I was walking and saw rabbits all
                                                   over the place.'

1. WOW VERY-BIG AIRPORT, HAVE AIRPLANE MANY.   (IN-A-ROW)

2. BEFORE NONE, NOW HAVE DEAF BUSINESS MANY.   (ALL-OVER)

3. I LOOK-AT, SEE BIRD 5.   (IN-A-ROW)

4. ARMY READY, IT HAVE AIRPLANE 25.   (IN-A-ROW)

5. PARTY FINISH, WOW BEER CAN MANY.   (ALL-OVER)

6. NOW PRICE HIGH, CAR NEW MANY CAN'T SELL.   (IN-A-ROW)

7. BEER CAN FATHER ENJOY COLLECT.   THERE HOME HAVE 150.   (IN-A-ROW)

Classifier: 1 Incorporating Number

The classifier CL:1 is used to show direction of movement of an upright human or animal. Note that the palm side of the CL:1 classifier represents the front of the human or animal.

EXAMPLES:

A. MAN CL:1-THERE-TO-HERE.   'The man came up to me.'

B. MAN CL:1-HERE-TO-THERE.   'The man walked away from me.'

C. MAN CL:1-THERE-TO-THERE.   'The man walked by.'

The CL:1 classifier can incorporate the numbers 1-5 to indicate the number of upright humans or animals in motion.

EXAMPLES:

D. CL:1(2)-THERE-TO-HERE BAWL-ME-OUT.   'The two of them came up to me and bawled me out.'

E. WOMAN CL:1(3)-THERE-TO-THERE.   'The three women passed by.'

Exercise 21.2:

Incorporate the number given in parentheses into the CL:1 classifier in the following sentences.

EXAMPLE:

STUDENT CL:1-THERE-TO-HERE COMPLAIN-REPEATEDLY.
'The student came up to me and complained.'
  (2)
     STUDENT CL:1(2)-THERE-TO-HERE COMPLAIN-REPEATEDLY.
     'The two students came up to me and complained.'

                  ____ n _____
1. CL:1-THERE-TO-THERE, I SEE~NONE.   (3)

2. GIRL CL:1-THERE-TO-HERE CHAT FINISH, CL:1-HERE-TO-THERE.   (2)

3. BOY CL:1-THERE-TO-HERE, DEMAND MONEY.   I SHOCK.   (5)

4. BEAR CL:1-THERE-TO-HERE, I HERE-RUN-THERE.   (2)

              _____ q _____ _____ whq _____
5. CAN I CL:1-HERE-TO-THERE, ASK-HIM TIME MEETING WHAT?   (4)

NOTE: Other Uses of Classifier:1

The classifier CL:1 can use different movements to show actions of upright humans or animals.

'to pass by quickly'	'to saunter by'

'to turn away'	'to stagger'

Both hands can form the CL:1 classifier to show the relative position of two or more upright humans or animals.

'to go up to another person or animal'	'the two of them go up to another person or animal'

'two of them follow another person or animal from behind'	'to approach a person, hesitate and walk away'

More Quantifiers

Some other classifiers which are used as quantifiers are:

CL: 44	CL:B	CL:BB

To mean many objects such as boyfriends, shirts, books.

To mean a small pile of objects such as dishes, food, homework.

To mean a large pile of objects such as clothes, furniture, many dishes.

These quantifiers may appear either before or after the noun, or at the end of the sentence.

EXAMPLES:

         t
A. FOOD CL:B, HE LIKE HE.　'He likes a lot of food.'

      t
CL:B FOOD, HE LIKE HE.　'He likes a lot of food.'
 t
FOOD, HE LIKE CL:B HE.　'He likes a lot of food.'

Exercise 21.3:

Form responses to the following questions using the classifier given in parentheses.

EXAMPLE:

           _____ q _____

Question: SHE HAVE BOY FRIEND?   'Does she have a boyfriend?'
           (CL:44)
Response: SHE HAVE CL:44   'She has many.'
          CL:44 HAVE SHE.   'She has many.'

    _____q_____
1. FOOD LEFT THERE?   (CL:B)
    _____ whq _____
2. FURNITURE YOU HAVE HOW-MUCH?   (CL:BB)
    _____q_____
3. DIRTY CLOTHES YOU HAVE?   (CL:BB)
    _____q_____
4. YOU TAKE MEAT FINISH YOU?   (CL:B)
    _____q_____
5. SHE HAVE DRESS MANY?   (CL:44)
    _____ whq _____
6. HOW-MANY PEOPLE THEY WANT BUY TICKET?   (CL:44)
    _____q_____
7. CLOTHES OLD, IT HAVE?   (CL:BB)

Vocabulary

ANOTHER, other

ARMY

ASSISTANT

BEAR

BLUSH

BRIDGE

CENTER, middle

CHANNEL, knob

CONNECT, belong, join

END, complete

FOREST

GENERAL, broad

GOOD-AT, skilled, expert

GOSSIP, rumor

HIGH

JUST, only

LINE

LOCK-UP

LOW, lower

MATCH, combine

MEAN, meaning

MELT, dissolve, fade

NEWS, information

OPERATE (on body),
surgery

PAINT
Noun: paint

PEACE

PLUG-IN
Noun: plug

PRETEND, fool

SECRET, private, confidential

SHOCK

SHOUT

SPECIAL, except

SPIRIT, soul, ghost

SUMMARIZE, condense, abbreviate

SUPERVISE

TEMPT

TRADE-PLACES-WITH, switch

WAR, battle

WONDER

Outlining for Shape and Detail

The tips of the index fingers can be used to outline the shape of an object or to show detail of an object.

EXAMPLES:

A. HOME HAVE TABLE OUTLINE-KIDNEY-SHAPED. 'I have a table at home that is kidney-shaped.'

B. FLOWER BOWL HAVE SCALLOPED-RIM. 'The flower bowl has a scalloped rim.'

C. HAVE PAPER OUTLINE-RECTANGLE THERE. 'There's a big piece of paper there.'

Exercise 22.1:

Outline and give detail of the objects in the following pictures.

Shaping Objects With Classifier:BB

The classifier:CL:BB can be used to describe the surface shape of an object.

EXAMPLES:

A. BED OLD HAVE CL:BB-DIP.   'The old bed has a dip in the middle.'

B. GRASS CL:BB-SLOPE. 'The lawn has a gentle slope.'

C. NEW-YORK THERE HAVE BUILDING CL:BB-TALL-SIDES.
'New York has many tall buildings.'

Exercise 22.2:

Use the classifier:CL:BB to describe the surface shapes of the objects in the following pictures.

Classifiers Showing Motion

Some classifiers can be used to show the motion of the humans, animals, or objects they represent.

EXAMPLES:

To mean a large quantity of people, cars, animals, etc., moving toward a specific location.

To mean a continuing stream of people or animals filing past.

To mean a continuing stream of objects filing along as on an assembly line such as newspapers on a conveyer belt.

To mean a flow of liquid such as a gas leak, a runny nose, running water, bleeding, etc.

EXAMPLES:

A. IT HAVE S-A-L-E PEOPLE CL:55↟↟.   'People were rushing to the sale.'

B. RESTAURANT PEOPLE CL:44 ⇉ IT GOOD IT.   'That restaurant is good, so many people go there.'

C. BEFORE WORK P-O, LETTER CL:44 ⇉ .   'I used to work at the post office sorting mail.'

D. WATER CL:4↓ GO-TO-IT FIX!   'The water's dripping, go fix it!'

Exercise 22.3:

Substitute each of the signs in the lists into the model sentence given.

EXAMPLE:

I SIT WATCH CHILDREN CL:44 ⇉ SCHOOL.
'I sat and watched the children going to school.'
   TEACHER
      I SIT WATCH TEACHER CL:44 ⇉ SCHOOL.
      'I sat and watched the teachers going to school.'

1. BEFORE I WORK FACTORY TOMATO CL:44⇉.
   COKE
   CAN
   FISH
   CAR

2. MEETING IMPORTANT PEOPLE CL:55⇡⇡.
   DEAF
   COP
   INTERPRETER
   RESEARCHER

3. #BUSY HE DAILY PEOPLE CL:44⇉ HIS ROOM.
   STUDENT
   SICK PEOPLE
   ACTOR
   BOY, GIRL

4. AWFUL ALL-NIGHT WATER CL:4↓ .
   #GAS
   NOSE
   TOILET
   ROOF

Vocabulary

AFRICA

APPROACH

AUSTRALIA

BAPTIST, baptize

BLIND

BOWL

#BUSY

CANADA

CATHOLIC

CHINA, Chinese

COMMUTE, go back and forth

CONGRATULATIONS

COOPERATE

EGYPT

ENGLAND, British, English

EPISCOPAL

FOREVER

FRANCE, French

#GAS

GERMANY, German

GOD

GRASS

GREECE, Greek

HOSPITAL, infirmary

INDIA, Indian

ISRAEL, Jewish

ITALY

JAPAN, Japanese

LUTHERAN

231

MEDICINE, chemical   METHODIST   MEXICO, Mexican

MORMON   NATIVE-AMERICAN, Indian   PROTESTANT

RELIGION, religious   ROOF   RUSSIA, Russian

SCOTLAND, Scottish   SPAIN, Spanish   TOMATO

DIALOGUE 7

Jack and Alice are discussing the television decoder.

Jack: I GET T-V CAPTION LAST-WEEK.   TRUE WONDERFUL.

Alice: I FINISH ORDER.   WAIT-CONTINUALLY, NOT-YET

 ___ whq _____
ARRIVE.   LOOK~LIKE WHAT?

Jack: CL:BB (flat) CL:BB (wide), METAL.   HAVE CL:F

 _____ if _____
CHANNEL.   SUPPOSE T-V NOW HAVE CAPTION, YOU O-N IT

C-A-P-T-I-O-N, FINISH IT T-V CAPTION.

Alice: THEY MAKE SEVERAL T-V CAPTION, WRONG PEOPLE

CL:55⚡ WANT.   THEY NOT EXPECT.   NOW START MORE

CL:44⇶ SELL-REPEATEDLY.

 _rq_
Jack: T-V CAPTION WORK HOW?   WELL, T-V HAVE CL:G+++

(downward), 1 CL:G THAT-ONE IT LINE 21.   IT HAVE

CAPTION.   MUST HAVE BOX, THAT-ONE T-V CAPTION, PLUG-IN

FINISH, WILL IT APPEAR CAPTION.

Alice: TRUE WONDERFUL.   I HURRY GET.

NOTES

234

THE MANUAL ALPHABET

NOTES

NUMBERS

zero

one

two

three

four

five

six

seven

eight

nine

ten

eleven

237

twelve

thirteen

fourteen

fifteen

sixteen

seventeen

eighteen

nineteen

twenty

twenty-one

twenty-two

twenty-three

twenty-four

 twenty-five

 thirty

 forty

 fifty

 sixty

 seventy

 eighty

 ninety

 one hundred

 one thousand

 one million

NOTES

REFERENCES

DEAF COMMUNITY AND DEAF CULTURE

Jacobs, L. 1969. *A Deaf Adult Speaks Out.* Washington, D.C.: Gallaudet College Press.

Kannapell, B. 1980. Personal awareness and advocacy in the deaf community. In C. Baker and R. Battison (eds.), *Sign Language and the Deaf Community.* Silver Spring, MD: National Association of the Deaf.

Lane, H. 1976. *The Wild Boy of Aveyron.* Cambridge, MA: Harvard University Press.

Lane, H. 1977. Notes for a psychohistory of American Sign Language. *Deaf American* 30:3–7.

Meadow, K. 1972. Sociolinguistics, Sign Language and the Deaf subculture. In T. O'Rourke (ed.), *Psycholinguistics and Total Communication: the State of the Art.* Silver Spring, MD: National Association of the Deaf.

Padden, C. and H. Markowicz 1976. Cultural conflicts between hearing and deaf communities. In *Proceedings of the Seventh World Congress of the World Federation of the Deaf.* Silver Spring, MD: National Association of the Deaf.

Padden, C. 1980. The deaf community and the culture of Deaf people. In C. Baker and R. Battison (eds.), *Sign Language and the Deaf Community.* Silver Spring, MD: National Association of the Deaf.

Woodward, J. 1978. Historical bases of American Sign Language. In P. Siple (ed.), *Understanding Language through Sign Language Research.* New York: Academic Press.

Woodward, J. 1980. Sociolinguistic research on American Sign Language: A historical perspective. In C. Baker and R. Battison (eds.), *Sign Language and the Deaf Community.* Silver Spring, MD: National Association of the Deaf.

AMERICAN SIGN LANGUAGE

Baker, C. 1977. Regulators and turn-taking in American Sign Language discourse. In L. Friedman (ed.), *On the Other Hand: New Perspectives in American Sign Language.* New York: Academic Press.

Baker, C. and C. Padden 1978. Focusing on the nonmanual components of American Sign Language. In P. Siple (ed.), *Understanding Language through Sign Language Research.* New York: Academic Press.

Baker, C. and C. Padden 1978. *American Sign Language: A Look at its History, Structure and Community.* Silver Spring, MD: TJ Publishers, Inc.

Baker, C. 1980. Sentences in American Sign Language. In C. Baker and R. Battison (eds.), *Sign Language and the Deaf Community.* Silver Spring, MD: National Association of the Deaf.

Battison, R. 1978. *Lexical Borrowing in American Sign Language.* Silver Spring, MD: Linstok Press.

Battison, R. 1980. Signs have parts: A simple idea. In C. Baker and R. Battison (eds.), *Sign Language and the Deaf Community.* Silver Spring, MD: National Association of the Deaf.

Bellugi, U. 1980. How signs express complex meanings. In C. Baker and R. Battison (eds.), *Sign Language and the Deaf Community.* Silver Spring, MD: National Association of the Deaf.

Cogen, C. 1977. On three aspects of time expression in American Sign Language. In L. Friedman (ed.), *On the Other Hand: New Perspectives on American Sign Language.* New York: Academic Press.

241

Fischer, S. and B. Gough 1978. Verbs in American Sign Language. *Sign Language Studies,* 18:17–48.

Frishberg, N. 1975. Arbitrariness and iconicity: Historical change in American Sign Language. *Language,* 51:676–710.

Klima, E. and U. Bellugi 1979. *The Signs of Language.* Cambridge, MA: Harvard University Press.

Liddell, S. 1978. Nonmanual signals and relative clauses in American Sign Language. In P. Siple (ed.), *Understanding Language through Sign Language Research.* New York: Academic Press.

Supalla, T. and E. Newport 1978. How many seats in a chair? The derivation of nouns and verbs in American Sign Language. In P. Siple (ed.), *Understanding Language through Sign Language Research.* New York: Academic Press.

Wilbur, R. 1979. *American Sign Language and Sign Systems.* Baltimore: University Park Press.

Woodward, J. and C. Erting 1974. Synchronic variation and historical change in American Sign Language. *Language Sciences,* 37:9–12.

ANSWER KEY

EXERCISE 1.1

1. YOU-PL.
2. THEY
3. I
4. HE/SHE/IT
5. THEY
6. YOU
7. THEY
8. WE

EXERCISE 1.2

1. YOU TALL YOU.   'You are tall.'
2. IT HEAVY IT.   'It is heavy.'
3. I SURPRISED I.   'I am surprised.'
4. THEY DEAF THEY.   'They are deaf.'
5. YOU HEARING YOU.   'You are hearing.'
6. I MAD I.   'I am mad.'
7. SHE SLEEPY SHE.   'She is sleepy.'
8. WE DEAF WE.   'We are deaf.'
9. IT LIGHT IT.   'It is light.'
10. YOU HAPPY YOU.   'You are happy.'
11. WE SURPRISED WE.   'We are surprised.'
12. HE INTERESTING HE.   'He is interesting.'
13. YOU PRETTY YOU.   'You are pretty.'
14. IT UGLY IT.   'It is ugly.'
15. I SHORT I.   'I am short.'
16. THEY SURPRISED THEY.   'They are surprised.'
17. IT BIG IT.   'It is big.'
18. I SLEEPY I.   'I am sleepy.'
19. IT SMALL IT.   'It is small.'
20. SHE DEAF SHE.   'She is deaf.'

EXERCISE 2.1

1. YOUR
2. HER
3. OUR
4. THEIR
5. YOUR-PL.
6. ITS
7. MY
8. HIS
9. HIS
10. THEIR

EXERCISE 2.2

1. SHE MY SISTER.   'She is my sister.'
2. HE MY BROTHER.   'He is my brother.'

243

3. HE YOUR FATHER. 'He is your father.'
4. HE OUR FATHER. 'He is our father.'
5. SHE MY GRANDMOTHER 'She is my grandmother.'
6. HE MY FRIEND. 'He is my friend.'
7. HE YOUR GRANDFATHER. 'He is your grandfather.'
8. HE YOUR TEACHER. 'He is your teacher.'
9. HE MY STUDENT. 'He is my student.'
10. HE MY FRIEND. 'He is my friend.'
11. HE BOY. 'He is a boy.'
12. SHE GIRL. 'She is a girl.'
13. HE MAN. 'He is a man.'
14. SHE WOMAN. 'She is a woman.'

EXERCISE 2.3

1. SHE HER SISTER SHE. 'She is her sister.'
2. SHE HER MOTHER SHE. 'She is her mother.'
3. SHE THEIR TEACHER SHE. 'She is their teacher.'
4. SHE HIS GRANDMOTHER SHE. 'She is his grandmother.'
5. HE HER FRIEND HE. 'He is her friend.'
6. HE HIS STUDENT HE. 'He is his student.'
7, HE HER BROTHER HE. 'He is her brother.'
8. HE HIS FATHER HE. 'He is his father.'
9. HE HER GRANDFATHER HE. 'He is her grandfather.'
10. SHE HIS SISTER SHE. 'She is his sister.'

EXERCISE 3.1

1. I FORGET BOOK I. 'I forgot a book.'
2. I REMEMBER BOOK I. 'I remember the book.'
3. I LIKE BOOK I. 'I like the book.'
4. I KNOW BOOK I. 'I know the book.'
5. I WANT BOOK I. 'I want a book.'
6. I HAVE BOOK I. 'I have a book.'
7. I READ BOOK I. 'I read a book.'
8. I LOSE BOOK I. 'I lost the book.'
9. I FIND BOOK I. 'I found a book.'
10. I ENJOY BOOK I. 'I enjoyed the book.'

EXERCISE 3.2

1. WOMAN SHE REMEMBER BOOK SHE. 'The woman remembers the book.'
2. WOMAN SHE REMEMBER YOUR NAME SHE. 'The woman remembers your name.'
3. WOMAN SHE FORGET YOUR NAME SHE. 'The woman forgot your name.'
4. WOMAN SHE FORGET YOUR BOOK SHE. 'The woman forgot your book.'
5. BOY HE FORGET YOUR BOOK HE. 'The boy forgot your book.'
6. BOY HE HAVE YOUR BOOK HE. 'The boy has your book.'
7. BOY HE HAVE YOUR PAPER HE. 'The boy has your paper.'
8. BOY HE NEED YOUR PAPER HE. 'The boy needs your paper.'
9. GIRL SHE NEED YOUR PAPER SHE. 'The girl needs your paper.'
10. GIRL SHE REMEMBER SIGN SHE. 'The girl remembers signs.'
11. MAN HE REMEMBER SIGN HE. 'The man remembers signs.'
12. MAN HE PRACTICE SIGN HE. 'The man practices signs.'
13. WOMAN SHE PRACTICE SIGN SHE. 'The woman practices signs.'
14. WOMAN SHE HAVE CHAIR SHE. 'The woman has a chair.'
15. WOMAN SHE NEED CHAIR SHE. 'The woman needs a chair.'

16. WOMAN SHE NEED CAR SHE. 'The woman needs a car.'
17. MAN HE NEED MONEY HE. 'The man needs money.'
18. MAN HE WANT MONEY HE. 'The man wants money.'
19. GIRL SHE WANT BOOK SHE. 'The girl wants a book.'
20. GIRL SHE HAVE BOOK SHE. 'The girl has a book.'

EXERCISE 3.3

1. I READ BOOK INTERESTING. 'I read an interesting book.'
2. HE HAVE HOME PRETTY HE. 'He has a pretty home.'
3. SHE WANT CHAIR BLUE. 'She wants a blue chair.'
4. I REMEMBER MAN TALL. 'I remember the tall man.'
5. HE LOSE BOOK GREEN HE. 'He lost a green book.'
6. THEY FIND BOX SMALL. 'They found a small box.'
7. HE WANT TABLE NEW. 'He wants a new table.'
8. I NEED PAPER YELLOW FOR CLASS I. 'I need yellow paper for class.'
9. I KNOW WOMAN DEAF I. 'I know a deaf woman.'
10. SHE LIKE CAR SMALL SHE. 'She likes the small car.'

EXERCISE 3.4

1. I READ INTERESTING BOOK. 'I read an interesting book.'
2. HE HAVE PRETTY HOME HE. 'He has a pretty home.'
3. SHE WANT BLUE CHAIR. 'She wants a blue chair.'
4. I REMEMBER TALL MAN. 'I remember the tall man.'
5. HE LOSE GREEN BOOK HE. 'He lost a green book.'
6. THEY FIND SMALL BOX. 'They found a small box.'
7. HE WANT NEW TABLE. 'He wants a new table.'
8. I NEED YELLOW PAPER FOR CLASS I. 'I need yellow paper for class.'
9. I KNOW DEAF WOMAN I. 'I know a deaf woman.'
10. SHE LIKE SMALL CAR SHE. 'She likes the small car.'

EXERCISE 3.5

1. IT CL:BB. 'It is long and flat.'
2. IT CL:ÏL. 'It is large, flat and round.'
3. IT CL:F. 'It is small, flat and round.'
4. IT CL:BB. 'It is long and flat.'
5. IT CL:BB. 'It is long and flat.'
6. IT CL:ÏL. 'It is quite large, flat and round.'
7. IT CL:C. 'It is small and container-like.'
8. IT CL:ÏL. 'It is quite large, flat and round.'
9. IT CL:CC. 'It is quite large and container-like.'
10. IT CL:ÏL. 'It is flat and round.'
11. IT CL:CC. 'It is large and container-like.'
12. IT CL:F. 'It is small, flat and round.'

EXERCISE 4.1

    _____n_____
1. HE DON'T-LIKE MOVIE HE. 'He doesn't like the movie.'
    _____n_____
2. DAUGHTER SHE DON'T-LIKE SCHOOL SHE. 'My daughter doesn't like school.'
    _____n_____
3. I NOT SEE DOG I. 'I don't see a dog.'

$\qquad$ —n————
4. IT SMELL GOOD NOT IT.   'It doesn't smell good.'
$\qquad$ ————————n————
5. I NOT UNDERSTAND BOOK I.   'I don't understand the book.'
$\qquad$ ————n————
6. THEY BELIEVE YOU NOT.   'They don't believe you.'
$\qquad$ ————n————
7. CAT IT NOT HUNGRY IT.   'The cat isn't hungry.'
$\qquad$ ————n————
8. HOUSE IT NOT EXPENSIVE IT.   'The house is not expensive.'
$\qquad$ ————n————
9. IT FOOD HOT NOT IT.   'The food is not hot.'
$\qquad$ ————————n————
10. WOMAN SHE DON'T-WANT T-T-Y SHE.   'The woman doesn't want a TTY.'
$\qquad$ ————n————
11. SHE DON'T-KNOW SIGN SHE.   'The woman doesn't know sign language.'
$\qquad$ ————n————
12. BOY HE LOSE MONEY NOT HE.   'The boy didn't lose the money.'
$\qquad$ ————n————
13. CAR IT BLUE NOT IT.   'The car isn't blue.'

EXERCISE 4.2

—n——
1. I TIRED I.   'I'm not tired.'
$\qquad$ ——n————
2. YOU UNDERSTAND ME.   'You don't understand me.'
$\qquad$ ——n————
3. GIRL HAVE BOOK SHE.   'The girl doesn't have the book.'
$\qquad$ ————n————
4. MY SISTER FIND MONEY.   'My sister didn't find the money.'
$\qquad$ ——n——
5. I SMELL IT I.   'I don't smell it.'
$\qquad$ ——n——
6. I WORK I.   'I don't work.'
$\qquad$ ————n————
7. THEY PRACTICE SIGN.   'They don't practice signs.'

EXERCISE 4.3

$\qquad$ — q ————
1. HE LIKE WORK HE?   'Does he like to work?'
$\qquad$ —— q ————
2. TEACHER LOSE MY PAPER?   'Did the teacher lose my paper?'
$\qquad$ —— q ————
3. IT HOUSE COLD IT?   'Is the house cold?'
$\qquad$ ——— q ————
4. GRANDMOTHER FIND MONEY?   'Did Grandmother find the money?'
$\qquad$ —— q ————
5. IT CAT HUNGRY IT?   'Is the cat hungry?'
$\qquad$ —— q ——
6. IT BOOK RIGHT IT?   'Is the book right?'
$\qquad$ ———— q ————
7. DOG IT UNDERSTAND SIGN IT?   'Does the dog understand signs?'
$\qquad$ —— q ————
8. SHE KNOW MY NAME SHE?   'Does she know my name?'

9. BOY HE SHORT HE? 'Is the boy short?'

_____ q _____
10. HE HEARING HE? 'Is he hearing?'

EXERCISE 4.4

_____ n _____
1. NO, HE DON'T-LIKE HE. 'No, he doesn't.'

_____ n _____
2. NO, HE NOT LOSE. 'No, he didn't.'

_____ y _____
3. YES, IT COLD IT. 'Yes, it is.'

_____ y ____
4. YES, SHE FIND. 'Yes, she did.'

_____ n _____
5. NO, IT NOT SICK IT. 'No, it isn't.'

_____ n ___
6. NO, IT NOT IT. 'No, it isn't.'

_____ y _____
7. YES, IT UNDERSTAND IT. 'Yes, it does.'

_____ y _____
8. YES, SHE KNOW SHE. 'Yes, she does.'

_____ y _____
9. YES, HE HEARING HE. 'Yes, he is.'

_____ n _____
10. NO, HE NOT HE. 'No, he's not.'

EXERCISE 4.5

_____ nq _____
1. YOU UNDERSTAND ME? 'You don't understand me?'

_____ nq _____
2. SHE SEE MOVIE NOT? 'She didn't see the movie?'

_____ nq ____
3. HE DEAF HE? 'He's not deaf?'

_____ nq _____
4. SHE DON'T-WANT CAT? 'She doesn't want the cat?'

_____ nq _____
5. HE DON'T-KNOW MY SISTER HE? 'He doesn't know my sister?'

_____ nq ___
6. IT DIRTY NOT IT? 'It's not dirty?'

_____ nq _____
7. HE NOT AMERICAN HE? 'He's not an American?'

DIALOGUE 1

Jack: Hello. Is she a friend of yours?
Tom: Yes. Her name is Betty Smith. She's from Indiana.
Jack: I'm happy to meet you. My name is Jack Jones. I'm from Minnesota.
Betty: I'm happy to meet you. Do you have a brother named Bob Jones?
Jack: Yes. Do you know him?
Betty: Yes, I know him.
Tom: Well, the deaf world is a small one!

EXERCISE 5.1

1. YESTERDAY I PRACTICE SIGN I. 'Yesterday I practiced my signs.'
2. RECENTLY HE BUY CAR HE. 'Recently, he bought a car.'
3. BEFORE BOY HE STUDENT HE. 'The boy was a student before.'
4. YESTERDAY SHE DIE SHE, SORRY. 'She died yesterday. I was sorry about it.'
5. LONG-AGO I TEACH RESIDENTIAL-SCHOOL I. 'I taught at a residential school a long time ago.'
6. RECENTLY WOMAN SHE LOSE P-I-N CL:F. 'Recently, the woman lost a round pin.'
   _____ n _____
7. YESTERDAY I NOT READ YOUR HOMEWORK. 'I didn't read your homework yesterday.'
8. RECENTLY HE LEARN SIGN HE. 'He learned sign language recently.'
9. BEFORE SHE HEARING SCHOOL. 'She went to a hearing school before.'
10. LONG-AGO SHE VISIT WASHINGTON SHE. 'She visited Washington a long time ago.'

EXERCISE 5.2

1. HE FATHER FINISH MAKE COOKIE HE. 'Father made cookies.'
2. SHE WRITE PAPER FINISH SHE. 'She wrote a paper.'
3. BROTHER FINISH READ BOOK HE. 'My brother has read the book.'
4. I FINISH SELL HOUSE I. 'I already sold the house.'
5. MOVIE I SEE FINISH I. 'I have seen the movie.'
6. I FINISH VISIT GRANDMOTHER I. 'I already visited Grandmother.'
7. MY SIGN FINISH IMPROVE. 'My sign language has already improved.'
8. HE FINISH DRINK WATER HE. 'He drank some water.'
9. SON HE GROW-UP FINISH HE. 'My son has grown up.'
10. I FINISH COOK ALL-DAY. 'I cooked all day.'

EXERCISE 5.3

1. TOMORROW I PRACTICE SIGN I. 'Tomorrow I will practice my signs.'
2. I WILL GO COLLEGE I. 'I will go to college.'
3. LATER I TO-TELEPHONE YOU I. 'I will telephone you later.'
4. HE LEARN SIGN WILL HE. 'He will learn sign language.'
5. COOKIE CL:L̈L I FUTURE MAKE I. 'I'll make a large cookie later on.'
6. AFTER-AWHILE T-T-Y SHE BUY SHE. 'After awhile, she will buy a TTY.'
7. TOMORROW I SEE MOVIE I. 'I'll see the movie tomorrow.'
8. PANTS I WILL WEAR I. 'I'll wear pants.'
9. MOTHER WILL STAY 1-WEEK. 'Mother will stay one week.'

EXERCISE 6.1

_t _
1. TEA I PREFER I. 'I prefer tea.'
_t _
2. TEA I HATE I. 'I hate tea.'
___t _
3. WORK I HATE I. 'I hate work.'
___t _
4. WORK I ENJOY I. 'I enjoy work.'
_t _
5. T-V I ENJOY I. 'I enjoy TV.'
_t _
6. T-V I LOOK-AT I. 'I watch TV.'
___t ___
7. BICYCLE I LOOK-AT I. 'I looked at the bicycle.'

248

   __ t __

8. BICYCLE I DON'T-LIKE I.   'I don't like the bicycle.'

   __ t _

9. MEAT I DON'T-LIKE I.   'I don't like meat.'

   __ t _

10. MEAT I NOT EAT I.   'I don't eat meat.'

   __ t __

11. SWEET I NOT EAT I.   'I don't eat sweets.'

   __ t _

12. SWEET I NOT BUY I.   'I don't buy sweets.'

EXERCISE 6.2

   __ t __

1. TICKET TOMORROW YOU-PAY-ME.   'I'll pay you for the ticket tomorrow.'

   __ t __

2. LETTER LATER YOU-SEND-ME. 'You send me the letter later.'

   _____ t _____

3. RIGHT ADDRESS TOMORROW YOU-TELL-ME.   'You tell me the right address tomorrow.'

   _____ t _____

4. TELETYPEWRITER NEW YOU-SHOW-ME WILL YOU.   'You will show me the new teletypewriter.'

5. YOU FINISH YOU-ASK-ME.   'You already asked me.'

   __ t __

6. LETTER YOU-HELP-ME WRITE WILL YOU.   'You will help me write the letter.'

7. YOU-GIVE-ME PICTURE NOW.   'You give me the picture now.'

8. AFTER-AWHILE YOU AGAIN YOU-ASK-ME.   'You ask me again after awhile.'

   _____ t _____

9. PRETTY CL:L̈L YOU-SHOW-ME WILL YOU.   'You will show me the pretty plate.'

   ___ t ___

10. UMBRELLA LONG-AGO YOU-GIVE-ME.   'You gave me the umbrella a long time ago.'

EXERCISE 6.3

1. YESTERDAY SHE-TELL-ME STAY.   'Yesterday she told me to stay.'

   __ t __

2. CLOTHES TOMORROW HE-HELP-ME BUY.   'He will help me buy clothes tomorrow.'

3. FINISH HE-ASK-ME WAIT.   'He already asked me to wait.'

   __ t _

4. MOVIE LATER SHE-SHOW-ME.   'She will show me the movie later.'

   __ t __

5. MONEY TOMORROW SHE-SEND-IT.   'She will send them (the company) money tomorrow.'

   _____ q _____

6. WILL HE-ASK-YOU WORK?   'Will he ask you to work?'

   _____ q _____

7. BREAD TODAY HE-HELP-YOU MAKE?   'Will he help you make bread today?'

   _____ t _____

8. NEW WRISTWATCH HE-SHOW-YOU NOW.   'He will show you the new watch now.'

   _ t _

9. BOX SHE-SEND-YOU LATER.   'She will send you the box later.'

EXERCISE 6.4

   _ t _

1. BOX GIVE-CL:C↑-YOU.   'I'll give you a box.'

   __ t __

2. PAPER GIVE-CL:C↑-YOU.   'I'll give you a stack of paper.'

249

    —t—
3. WATER GIVE-CL:C-YOU. 'I'll give you a glass of water.'
    —t—
4. BOOK GIVE-CL:C↑-YOU. 'I'll give you a book.'
    —t—
5. GLASS GIVE-CL:C-YOU. 'I'll give you a glass.'
    —t—
6. BOTTLE GIVE-CL:C-YOU. 'I'll give you a bottle.'
    —t—
7. PLANT GIVE-CL:C-YOU. 'I'll give you a potted plant.'
    —t—
8. COKE GIVE-CL:C-YOU. 'I'll give you a coke.'

EXERCISE 7.1

1. TOMORROW YOU-GIVE-ME MONEY! 'Give me the money tomorrow!'
    —t—
2. LETTER YOU-SEND-HER MOTHER! 'Send Mother a letter!'
    —t—
3. T-T-Y BUY YOU! 'Buy a TTY!'
4. PRACTICE SIGN YOU! 'Practice signing!'
5. REMEMBER SIGN YOU! 'Remember the signs!'
6. TOMORROW AGAIN YOU-TELL-HER! 'Tell her again tomorrow!'
7. ADVERTISEMENT YOU-SEND-ME! 'Send me the advertisement!'
8. PAY-ATTENTION YOU! 'Pay attention!'

EXERCISE 7.2

1. I FIND 3 GLASS. 'I found 3 glasses.'
2. I FIND COAT 1. 'I found 1 coat.'
3. I FIND 5 PENCIL. 'I found 5 pencils.'
4. I FIND STAMP 2. 'I found 2 stamps.'
5. I FIND 4 KNIFE. 'I found 4 knives.'
6. I FIND SPOON 3. 'I found 3 spoons.'
7. TOMORROW BROTHER OLD 4. 'Tomorrow my brother will be 4 years old.'
8. TOMORROW BROTHER OLD 9. 'Tomorrow my brother will be 9 years old.'
9. TOMORROW BROTHER OLD 6. 'Tomorrow my brother will be 6 years old.'
10. TOMORROW BROTHER OLD 2. 'Tomorrow my brother will be 2 years old.'
11. TOMORROW BROTHER OLD 5. 'Tomorrow my brother will be 5 years old.'
12. TOMORROW BROTHER OLD 1. 'Tomorrow my brother will be 1 year old.'
13. FRIEND WILL SHE-MEET-ME TIME 9. 'My friend will meet me at 9 o'clock.'
14. FRIEND WILL SHE-MEET-ME TIME 8. 'My friend will meet me at 8 o'clock.'
15. FRIEND WILL SHE-MEET-ME TIME 4. 'My friend will meet me at 4 o'clock.'
16. FRIEND WILL SHE-MEET-ME TIME 6. 'My friend will meet me at 6 o'clock.'
17. FRIEND WILL SHE-MEET-ME TIME 1. 'My friend will meet me at 1 o'clock.'
18. FRIEND WILL SHE-MEET-ME TIME 7. 'My friend will meet me at 7 o'clock.'

EXERCISE 7.3

1. THREE-OF-US PLAN GO-AWAY. 'We (the three of us) plan to go.'
2. FIVE-OF-US PLAN GO-AWAY. 'We (the five of us) plan to go.'
3. TWO-OF-YOU PLAN GO-AWAY. 'You (the two of you) plan to go.'
4. FOUR-OF-US PLAN GO-AWAY. 'We (the four of us) plan to go.'
5. FIVE-OF-THEM GO-WITH WILL. 'They (the five of them) will go together.'
6. FOUR-OF-US GO-WITH WILL. 'We (the four of us) will go together.'
7. TWO-OF-THEM GO-WITH WILL. 'They (the two of them) will go together.'
8. THREE-OF-YOU GO-WITH WILL. 'You (the three of you) will go together.'

EXERCISE 7.4

1. HE GROW-UP RABBIT 10 HE. 'He raised 10 rabbits.'
2. SON HE NEED PANTS MANY HE. 'My son needs many pairs of pants.'
3. SHE ORDER HAMBURGER 2 SHE. 'She ordered 2 hamburgers.'
4. I ORDER FRENCH-FRIES 3 I. 'I ordered 3 french fries.'
5. IT STORE HAVE SHOES MANY IT. 'The store has many pairs of shoes.'
6. STUDENT HE HAVE MISTAKE A-FEW HE. 'The student has a few mistakes.'
7. SHE FINISH SHE-GIVE-ME PICTURE SEVERAL. 'She gave me several pictures.'
8. I FINISH I-MEET-HER NEW NEIGHBOR SEVERAL. 'I have met several new neighbors.'
   _____ n _____
9. TWO-OF-THEM NOT HAVE FRIEND MANY. 'They don't have many friends.'
10. PEOPLE A-FEW STILL WAIT. 'A few people are still waiting.'

DIALOGUE 2

Jack: Do you know my brother?
Betty: Yes, I have met him. My sister and your brother are good friends.
Jack: I didn't know your sister is Deaf.
Betty: She is Deaf. Her name is Mary Williams.
Jack: I'm surprised. I know her. The last time I saw her was six years ago.
Betty: I have many pictures of Mary. I will give some to you.
Jack: Fine. I want to see them.

EXERCISE 8.1

    _____ whq _____
1. ARRIVE YESTERDAY WHAT? 'What arrived yesterday?'
    _____ whq _____
    T-T-Y ARRIVE WHEN? 'When did the TTY arrive?'
    _____ whq _____
2. LOSE SUITCASE WHO? 'Who lost a suitcase?'
    _____ whq_____
    AUNT LOSE WHAT? 'What did my aunt lose?'
    _____ whq _____
    AUNT LOSE SUITCASE WHEN? 'When did my aunt lose her suitcase?'
    _____ whq_____
    AUNT LOSE SUITCASE WHICH? 'Which suitcase did my aunt lose?'
    _____ whq _____
3. NOW VISIT S-D WHO? 'Who is visiting San Diego now?'
    _____ whq _____
    WIFE NOW VISIT WHERE? 'Where is your wife visiting now?'
    _____ whq _____
    WIFE NOW VISIT S-D WHAT-FOR? 'Why is your wife now visiting San Diego?'
    _____ whq _____
    WIFE NOW VISIT S-D WHY? 'Why is your wife now visiting San Diego?'
    _____ whq _____
4. HORSE ESCAPE HOW? 'How did the horse escape?'
    _____ whq _____
    HORSE ESCAPE WHEN? 'When did the horse escape?'
    _____whq _____
    HORSE ESCAPE WHICH? 'Which horse escaped?'

_____ whq _____

5. T-V BREAK WHEN? 'When did the TV break?'
_____ whq _____
BREAK LONG-AGO WHAT? 'What broke a long time ago?'
_____ whq _____
T-V BREAK HOW? 'How did the TV break?'

EXERCISE 8.2

_____ whq _____
1. WHAT ARRIVE YESTERDAY? 'What arrived yesterday?'
_____ whq _____
WHAT ARRIVE YESTERDAY WHAT? 'What arrived yesterday?'
_____ whq _____
WHEN T-T-Y ARRIVE? 'When did the TTY arrive?'
_____ whq _____
WHEN T-T-Y ARRIVE WHEN? 'When did the TTY arrive?'
_____ whq _____
2. WHO LOSE SUITCASE? 'Who lost a suitcase?'
_____ whq _____
WHO LOSE SUITCASE WHO? 'Who lost a suitcase?'
_____ whq _____
WHAT AUNT LOSE? 'What did my aunt lose?'
_____ whq _____
WHAT AUNT LOSE WHAT? 'What did my aunt lose?'
_____ whq _____
WHEN AUNT LOSE SUITCASE? 'When did my aunt lose her suitcase?'
_____ whq _____
WHEN AUNT LOSE SUITCASE WHEN? 'When did my aunt lose her suitcase?'
_____ whq _____
WHICH SUITCASE AUNT LOSE? 'Which suitcase did my aunt lose?'
_____ whq _____
WHICH SUITCASE AUNT LOSE WHICH? 'Which suitcase did my aunt lose?'
_____ whq _____
3. WHO NOW VISIT S-D? 'Who is visiting San Diego now?'
_____ whq _____
WHO NOW VISIT S-D WHO? 'Who is visiting San Diego now?'
_____ whq _____
WHERE WIFE NOW VISIT? 'Where is your wife visiting now?'
_____ whq _____
WHERE WIFE NOW VISIT WHERE? 'Where is your wife visiting now?'
_____ whq _____
WHAT-FOR WIFE NOW VISIT S-D? 'Why is your wife now visiting San Diego?'
_____ whq _____
WHAT-FOR WIFE NOW VISIT S-D WHAT-FOR? 'Why is your wife now visiting San Diego?'
_____ whq _____
WHY WIFE NOW VISIT S-D? 'Why is your wife now visiting San Diego?'
_____ whq _____
WHY WIFE NOW VISIT S-D WHY? 'Why is your wife now visiting San Diego?'
_____ whq _____
4. HOW HORSE ESCAPE? 'How did the horse escape?'
_____ whq _____
HOW HORSE ESCAPE HOW? 'How did the horse escape?'
_____ whq _____   _____
WHEN HORSE ESCAPE? 'When did the horse escape?'
_____ whq _____
WHEN HORSE ESCAPE WHEN? 'When did the horse escape?'

_____ whq _____
WHICH HORSE ESCAPE?   'Which horse escaped?'
_____ whq _____
WHICH HORSE ESCAPE WHICH?   'Which horse escaped?'
_____ whq _____
5. WHEN T-V BREAK?   'When did the TV break?'
_____ whq _____
WHEN T-V BREAK WHEN?   'When did the TV break?'
_____ whq _____
WHAT BREAK LONG-AGO?   'What broke a long time ago?'
_____ whq _____
WHAT BREAK LONG-AGO WHAT?   'What broke a long time ago?'
_____ whq _____
HOW T-V BREAK?   'How did the TV break?'
_____ whq _____
HOW T-V BREAK HOW?   'How did the TV break?'

EXERCISE 8.3

_____ y _____
1. YES, SHE DRAW HERSELF.   'Yes, she drew it herself.'
_____ y _____
2. YES, I I-TELL-HIM MYSELF.   'Yes, I'll tell him myself.'
_____ y _____
3. YES, I CLEAN-UP MYSELF.   'Yes, I cleaned it up myself.'
_____ y _____
4. YES, THEY DECIDE WRITE THEMSELVES.   'Yes, they decided to write it themselves.'
_____ y _____
5. YES, HE WRITE HIMSELF.   'Yes, he wrote it himself.'
_____ y _____
6. YES, HE BUILD HIMSELF.   'Yes, he built it himself.'
_____ y _____
7. YES, I GROW MYSELF.   'Yes, I grew them myself.'
_____ y ____
8. YES, HE WASH HIMSELF.   'Yes, he washed it himself.'

EXERCISE 8.4

_____ t ___ _____ n _____
1. TYPEWRITER MYSELF NOT HAVE.   'I don't have a typewriter.'
2. HIMSELF LONELY HE.   'He's lonely.'
3. HERSELF HAVE SKILL.   'She has the ability.'
_____ n _____
4. THEMSELVES ENTHUSIASTIC STUDY NOT.   'They're not eager to study.'
_____ q _____
5. TEST YOURSELF WORRY YOU?   'Are you worried about the test?'
_____ q _____
6. ANY QUESTION YOURSELF HAVE?   'Do you have any questions?'

EXERCISE 9.1

_____ y _____
1. COP SHE-GIVE-HIM TICKET.   'The cop gave him a ticket.'
_____ y _____
2. YES, TOMORROW TIME 3 HAVE MEETING.   'Yes, there's a meeting at 3 o'clock tomorrow.'

_____ y _____
3. YES, I HAVE NEW BICYCLE.   'Yes, I have a new bicycle.'
_____ n _____
4. NO, I NEED GAS.   'No, I need gas.'
_____ y _____
5. I HAVE HEARING-AID.   'Yes, I have a hearing aid.'
_____ n _____
6. NOT TO-TELEPHONE, TELEPHONE BREAK.   'Don't call, the telephone is broken.'
_____ y _____
7. YES, I HAVE TYPEWRITER.   'Yes, I have a typewriter.'
_____ n _____
8. I NOT HAVE KEY.   'I don't have the key.'
_____ n _____
9. I NOT HAVE BOOK.   'I don't have a book.'
10. I WANT AIRPLANE.   'I want (to use) an airplane.'

EXERCISE 9.2

__ t _____
1. GIRLFRIEND HAVE BLOND HAIR.   'My girlfriend, she has blond hair.'
__ t _____
2. CALIFORNIA WOW NICE.   'California, it's very nice.'
__ t __
3. TEACHER SHE-BAWL-OUT-HIM.   'The teacher, she bawled him out.'
_ t _
4. RAIN STOP.   'The rain, it stopped.'
___ t __
5. LEADER SHE-ASK-ME QUESTION.   'The leader, she asked me a question.'
____ t _____
6. HIS WRIST-WATCH STEAL.   'His wrist watch, it was stolen.'
_ t _ ____ n _____
7. TREE IT NOT LOOK GOOD.   'The tree, it doesn't look good.'
___ t _____
8. PERFORMANCE WONDERFUL.   'The performance, it was wonderful.'
_ t __
9. PLANT NEED WATER.   'The plant, it needs water.'
___ t __
10. MEETING CANCEL.   'The meeting, it was cancelled.'

EXERCISE 10.1

1. SHE SEE DOCTOR SHOULD SHE.   'She should see a doctor.'
_____ q _____
2. LETTER YOU GET WILL YOU?   'Will you get a letter?'
3. TOMORROW PRESIDENT APPEAR MAYBE.   'The president may show up tomorrow.'
4. HE RECOVER WILL HE.   'He'll get well.'
5. I WIN RACE MUST I.   'I must win the race.'
6. I LIPREAD CAN.   'I can lipread.'
7. LETTER I TYPE 1-MINUTE CAN I.   'I can type a letter in a minute.'
8. S-F YOU VISIT MUST YOU.   'You must visit San Francisco.'
9. HE TAKE-UP MORE CLASS SHOULD HE.   'He should take more classes.'
10. SISTER MARRY WILL.   'My sister will get married.'

EXERCISE 10.2

1. SHE SHOULD SEE DOCTOR SHE.   'She should see a doctor.'
_____ q _____
2. LETTER YOU WILL GET YOU?   'Will you get a letter?'

3. TOMORROW PRESIDENT MAYBE APPEAR.   'The president may show up tomorrow.'
4. HE WILL RECOVER HE.   'He'll get well.'
5. I MUST WIN RACE I.   'I must win the race.'
6. I CAN LIPREAD.   'I can lipread.'
7. LETTER I CAN TYPE 1-MINUTE I.   'I can type a letter in a minute.'
8. S-F YOU MUST VISIT YOU.   'You must visit San Francisco.'
9. HE SHOULD TAKE-UP MORE CLASS HE.   'He should take more classes.'
10. SISTER WILL MARRY.   'My sister will get married.'

EXERCISE 10.3

     ————— n —————
1. I STAY 1-HOUR CAN'T I.   'I can't stay an hour.'
     ————— n —————————
2. HE ACCEPT RESPONSIBILITY REFUSE HE.   'He won't take responsibility.'
     ————— n —————
3. HE NOT-YET COOK FOOD HE.   'He hasn't cooked the food.'
     ————— n —————
4. I GET-UP TIME 6 CAN'T I.   'I can't get up at six.'
     ————————— n —————————
5. TELEPHONE NUMBER HE MEMORIZE NOT-YET HE.   'He hasn't memorized the telephone
                                                number.'
     ————————— n —————
6. SHE BORN BABY NOT-YET SHE.   'She hasn't had her baby yet.'
     ————————— n —————
7. MAN HE HE-PAY-ME REFUSE HE.   'The man refuses to pay me.'
     ————————— n —————
8. LETTER HE-SEND-ME NOT-YET HE.   'He hasn't sent me a letter.'
     ————————— n —————
9. I NOT-YET TRY ESTABLISH C-L-U-B I.   'I haven't tried setting up a club.'
     ————————— n —————————
10. ADDRESS SHE PUT-DOWN FOR-YOU CAN'T SHE.   'She can't write down the address for you.'

EXERCISE 10.4

     ——— n ———
1. NO, I CAN'T I.   'No, I can't.'
     ——— y ———
2. YES, SHE SHOULD.   'Yes, she should.'
     ——— y ———
3. YES, I MAYBE I.   'Yes, I may.'
     ——— y ———
4. YES, YOU CAN.   'Yes, you can.'
     ——— n ———
5. NO, HE NOT-YET HE.   'No, he hasn't.'
     ——— y ———
6. YES, SHE FINISH.   'Yes, she did.'
     ——— y ———
7. YES, YOU SHOULD.   'Yes, you should.'
     ——— y ———
8. YES, HE MAYBE HE.   'Yes, he may.'
     ——— y ———
9. YES, SHE WILL SHE.   'Yes, she will.'

DIALOGUE 3

Jack: I just saw an interesting movie. It's an old movie, a sign presentation by George Veditz. Have you seen it?

Tom: No, I haven't. Who is this Veditz?

Jack: He was deaf, and was president of the N.A.D. back in 1913. You can see that his signs are older and different.

Tom: Why was the movie made?

Jack: The N.A.D. raised 5,000 dollars to make movies. They wanted to preserve and protect sign language for future generations of deaf people.

Tom: I'd like to see the movie. Where is it?

Jack: The library should have it. Ask your library.

EXERCISE 11.1

1. MY HOME HERE. 'My home is here.'
   MY HOME THERE. 'My home is over there.'
2. YOUR GLASSES HERE. 'Your glasses are here.'
   YOUR GLASSES THERE. 'Your glasses are over there.'
3. CAR HERE. 'The car is here.'
   CAR THERE. 'The car is over there.'
4. COKE MACHINE HERE. 'The coke machine is here.'
   COKE MACHINE THERE. 'The coke machine is over there.'
5. WOMAN HERE. 'The woman is here.'
   WOMAN THERE. 'The woman is over there.'
6. STORE HERE. 'The store is here.'
   STORE THERE. 'The store is over there.'
7. BASEBALL GAME HERE. 'The baseball game is here.'
   BASEBALL GAME THERE. 'The baseball game is over there.'
8. CHURCH OLD HERE. 'The old church is here.'
   CHURCH OLD THERE. 'The old church is over there.'
9. PAPER HERE. 'The paper is here.'
   PAPER THERE. 'The paper is over there.'
10. YOUR FRIEND HERE. 'Your friend is here.'
    YOUR FRIEND THERE. 'Your friend is over there.'

EXERCISE 11.2

1. BEFORE I WALK-THERE I. 'I walked there before.'
2. BEFORE I FLY-THERE I. 'I flew there before.'
3. FURNITURE HEAVY SHE MOVE-THERE. 'She moved the heavy furniture there.'
4. BEFORE YOU DRIVE-HERE YOU. 'You drove here before.'
5. BEFORE YOU WALK-HERE YOU. 'You walked here before.'
6. BEFORE YOU FLY-HERE YOU. 'You flew here before.'
7. BOOK MANY SHE PUT-HERE. 'She put many books here.'
8. CHICAGO, L-A HE THERE-DRIVE-THERE HE. 'He drove from Chicago to Los Angeles.'
9. CHICAGO, L-A HE THERE-FLY-THERE HE. 'He flew from Chicago to Los Angeles.'
10. STORE, YOUR HOME SHE THERE-DRIVE-THERE. 'She drove from the store to your home.'
11. STORE, YOUR HOME SHE THERE-BRING-THERE. 'She brought it from the store to your home.'

EXERCISE 11.3

1. CHICAGO HE MOVE-THERE, STAY 2 YEAR FINISH
   HE THERE-MOVE-THERE WASHINGTON. 'He moved to Chicago, stayed there for two years then he moved from there to Washington.'

2. C-F NOW I GIVE-YOU FINISH
YOU-GIVE-HIM TOMORROW.   'I'll give you the captioned film now then you can give it to him tomorrow.'
3. I STAY-HERE 1-WEEK WITH SISTER FINISH
I GO-THERE VISIT MOTHER.   'I'm staying here for a week with my sister, then I'll go and visit my mother.'
4. BREAKFAST I COOK FINISH YOU
WASH-DISH.   'I'll cook breakfast, then you can wash the dishes.'
5. SUITCASE I PACK FINISH I GO-THERE AIRPORT.   'I'll pack my suitcase then I'm going to the airport.'
6. PERFORMANCE PRACTICE ALL-DAY FINISH
TONIGHT HAVE PARTY THERE MY HOME.   'We'll practice our play all day then tonight there'll be a party at my home.'

EXERCISE 12.1

1. IT RESTAURANT HAVE FOOD.   'There's food at the restaurant.'
2. IT HOME HAVE TEA.   'There's tea at home.'
3. IT STORE HAVE SHOES.   'There are shoes at that store.'
4. IT SCHOOL HAVE DEAF STUDENT.   'There are deaf students at that school.'
5. IT RESTAURANT HAVE MEAT.   'There's meat at that restaurant.'
6. IT KITCHEN HAVE TABLE.   'There's a table in that kitchen.'
7. IT HOUSE HAVE CHAIR.   'There's a chair in the house.'
8. IT RESTAURANT HAVE RESTROOM.   'There's a restroom in the restaurant.'
9. IT R-E-F HAVE CREAM.   'There's cream in the refrigerator.'
10. IT BOOK HAVE SIGN.   'There are (pictures of) signs in the book.'

EXERCISE 12.2

1. WOMAN CL:Λ-THERE, SHE-LOOK-AT-ME.   'The woman stood over there and looked at me.'
2. I ENTER, LETTER CL:B-THERE.   'I went in, and the letter was lying there.'
3. SHOULD BICYCLE CL:3-THERE.   'The bicycle should be parked there.'
4. SURPRISED ME. PRESIDENT CL:Λ-HERE.   'I was surprised! The President was standing right next to me.'
      _____ t _____
5. CAR BLUE CL:3-THERE, THAT-ONE HIS.   'The blue car parked over there, that's his.'
6. SHE FORGET LEAVE MAGAZINE CL:B-THERE.   'She forgot and left the magazine lying there.'
7. RECENTLY BROTHER CL:Λ-HERE, NOW GONE.   'My brother was just standing right here, and now he's gone.'
8. CAR CL:3-THERE, NOW PUT-IN-GAS.   'The car is standing over there and now they're putting in some gas.'

EXERCISE 12.3

1. I SEE BEER CL:C-ON-TOP-OF-CL:B.   'I saw a beer can on top of the table.'
2. I SEE CAR CL:3-UNDER-CL:B.   'I saw a car parked in the garage.'
3. I SEE PAPER CL:B-NEXT-TO-CL:B.   'I saw two sheets of paper next to each other.'
4. I SEE PEOPLE CL:Λ-BEHIND-CL:Λ.   'I saw two people standing in line.'
5. I SEE PLANT CL:C-AND-CL:C-ON-TOP-OF-CL:B.   'I saw two small potted plants on a shelf.'
6. I SEE CL:F-NEXT-TO-CL:F.   'I saw two bottle tops next to each other.'
7. I SEE WOMAN CL:Λ-UNDER-CL:B.   'I saw a woman under an awning.'

EXERCISE 13.1

1. HE CRAZY-FOR CHEESE, HAVE PLENTY I.   'He really likes cheese and I've got plenty.'

      ___ t ___
2. SPORTS RESIDENTIAL-SCHOOL HAVE SOME. 'The school for the deaf has some sports.'
      ___ t _
3. WATER CALIFORNIA NOW HAVE PLENTY. 'California now has plenty of water.'
      ___ t _
4. MEAT IT HAVE LEFT IT A-LITTLE. 'There is a little meat left.'
      ____ t __
5. YOUR PIE GRANDMOTHER WANT SOME. 'Grandmother wants some of your pie.'

EXERCISE 13.2

1. DOG IT WANT CL:L̈ WATER. 'The dog wants a lot of water.'
2. MY HOUSE WOW DIRTY. HAVE CL:G D-U-S-T. 'My house is very dirty with a lot of dust.'
3. BASEMENT, I FIND CL:BB↑↓WATER. 'I found a lot of water in the basement!'
4. YESTERDAY, CL:BB↑↓ PAPER I THROW-AWAY. 'I threw away a pile of papers yesterday.'
5. CL:L̈ O-J YOU DRINK SHOULD YOU. 'You should drink a lot of orange juice.'
6. RECENTLY HE-GIVE-ME CL:BB↑↓ LETTER. 'He gave me a stack of letters recently.'
7. RAIN STOP FINISH, LEFT M-U-D CL:L̈. 'The rain left a lot of mud when it stopped.'

EXERCISE 13.3

1. STORE IT HAVE CL:5̈5̈ BICYCLE. 'The store has a large number of bicycles.'
2. H-O-T-E-L IT HAVE DOOR++. 'The hotel has many doors.'
3. MY SISTER FINISH HAVE CL:5̈5̈ BOYFRIEND. 'My sister already has a large number of boy-
                                       friends.'
4. I LIKE HOUSE WITH WINDOW++. 'I like houses with many windows.'
5. THERE PARTY I SEE CL:5̈5̈ CHILDREN. 'I saw a large number of children at the party.'
6. I MUST WRITE LIST++. 'I must write many lists.'
7. HE HAVE BEAUTIFUL GLASS++. 'He has many beautiful glasses.'

EXERCISE 13.4

      ___ t ___
1. BIRTHDAY HE-GIVE-ME 7-DOLLAR. 'He gave me 7 dollars for my birthday.'
2. I FIND 50-CENT YESTERDAY I. 'I found 50 cents yesterday.'
3. I WIN 300 DOLLAR I. 'I won 300 dollars.'
4. LONG-AGO T-T-Y COST 40 DOLLAR. 'A long time ago TTY's cost 40 dollars.'
5. LONG-AGO I BUY PENCIL COST 4-CENT. 'I used to buy pencils for 4 cents.'
      ____ t _____
6. MY CAR OLD SELL 450 DOLLAR. 'I sold my old car for 450 dollars.'
      _____ q _____
7. 20-DOLLAR YOU NEED TODAY? 'Do you need the 20 dollars today?'

DIALOGUE 4

Bill: Did you know there's a new play? A Deaf theatre group has been established in Los Angeles. Do
         you want to see it?
Jack: Yes, I would like to. Are there any seats left?
Bill: There should be a lot left. I will call them and reserve seats for the two of us. The tickets cost 3
         dollars each.
Jack: I can pay you now. Do you want to drive up there together?
Bill: Fine. We can watch the play then go to a friend's house for a party, talk with some friends then
         come on home.
Jack: What time should I meet you tomorrow?
Bill: At four o'clock. We will have plenty of time to drive up there.

EXERCISE 14.1

```
           _____n_____
1. I NONE HEAR YOU MARRY YOU.   'I didn't hear you got married.'
           _____n_____
   I HEAR ~NONE YOU MARRY YOU.   'I didn't hear you got married.'
       _____t_____   _____n_____
2. NURSE GIVE-SHOT, I NONE FEEL I.   'I felt nothing when the nurse gave me a shot.'
       _____t_____   ____n_____
   NURSE GIVE-SHOT, I FEEL ~NONE I.   'I felt nothing when the nurse gave me a shot.'
   __t____ _____n_____
3. WRENCH STORE IT NONE HAVE.   'The store doesn't have a wrench.'
   __t____ _____n_____
   WRENCH STORE IT HAVE ~NONE.   The store doesn't have a wrench.'
           _____n_____
4. IT C-O NONE HAVE DEAF WORK.   'The company doesn't have any Deaf workers.'
               _____n_____
   IT C-O HAVE ~NONE DEAF WORK.   'The company doesn't have any Deaf workers.'
           _____n_____
5. MAN NEVER INTERACT DEAF HE.   'The man never associates with Deaf people.'
           _____n_____
   MAN INTERACT DEAF NEVER HE.   'The man never associates with Deaf people.'
   _t_ _____n____
6. C-F HE NONE GET HE.   'He didn't get the captioned film.'
   _t_ _____n_____
   C-F HE GET NONE HE.   'He didn't get the captioned film.'
   ____t__ __n_____
7. TURKEY I NONE EAT.   'I didn't eat any turkey.'
   __t___ __n_____
   TURKEY I EAT ~NONE.   'I didn't eat any turkey.'
           _____t_____  ___n_____
8. MONEY YOU-GIVE-HER, I NONE SEE I.   'I didn't see the money you gave her.'
           _____t_____  ___n_____
   MONEY YOU-GIVE-HER, I SEE ~NONE I.   'I didn't see the money you gave her.'
       _____t_____ _____n_____
9. WOMAN SHE NEVER SHE-HELP-ME SHE.   'The woman never helped me.'
       _____t_____ _____n_____
   WOMAN SHE SHE-HELP-ME NEVER SHE.   'The woman never helped me.'
   _t_ _____n_____
10. T-V I NONE UNDERSTAND I.   'I can't understand the television at all.'
   _t_ _____n_____
   T-V I UNDERSTAND ~NONE I.   'I can't understand the television at all.'
       _____n_____
11. HE NEVER BATHE HE.   'He never bathes.'
       _____n_____
   HE BATHE NEVER HE.   'He never bathes.'
```

EXERCISE 14.2

```
       _____n_____
1. SHE BUY NOTHING.   'She bought nothing.'
           _____n_____
2. NOW YEAR, I GROW NOTHING.   'I didn't grow anything this year.'
       _____t_____  _____n_____
3. NURSE GIVE-SHOT, I FEEL NOTHING I.   'I felt nothing when the nurse gave me a shot.'
```

259

_____ n _____

4. NONE PEOPLE RIDE B-U-S.   'No one rides the bus.'

_ t _____ n _____

5. Z-O-O IT HAVE NONE MONKEY.   'There are no monkeys at the zoo.'

_____ n _____

6. I MUST SHOP, HAVE NONE FOOD LEFT.   'I have no food left so I must shop.'

____ t ____ _____ n _____

7. WORK P-O, HE EARN NOTHING.   'He makes nothing working at the post office.'

_____ n _____

8. REALLY I-INFORM-YOU, HAVE NONE TIME I.   'Really I must tell you I have no time.'

_____ n _____

9. YESTERDAY FRIEND HE LEARN NONE SIGN.   'My friend didn't learn any signs yesterday.'

_ t _____ n _____

10. A-A-A-D, I DO-WORK NOTHING.   'I didn't do anything for the American Athletic Association of the Deaf.'

EXERCISE 14.3

_____ t _____ _____ n _____

1. LETTER SHE-SEND-HIM, NOTHING SHE.   'She didn't send him the letter.'

_____ t _____ _____ n ___

2. SHIRT NEW WASH-IN-MACHINE, NOTHING I.   'I didn't wash the new shirt in the machine.

_____ t _____ _____ n ___

3. I RESPONSIBLE CAR-ACCIDENT, NOTHING I.   'I am not responsible for the car accident.'

_____ t _____ _____ n ___

4. I I-TTY-YOU YESTERDAY NIGHT, NOTHING I.   'I didn't call you on the TTY last night.'

_____ t _____ ____ n ___

5. I I-WARN-HIM FINISH, NOTHING I.   'I didn't warn him.'

____ t _____ ____ n ___

6. I-BOTHER-HIM, NOTHING I.   'I wasn't bothering him.'

_____ t _____ ____ n _____

7. BOY STEAL CAMERA, NOTHING HE.   'The boy didn't steal the camera.'

EXERCISE 15.1

_____ q _____

1. DON'T-MIND I-BORROW-HER DICTIONARY?   'Do you mind if I borrow her dictionary?'

_____ n _____

2. I UNDERSTAND. I DON'T-WANT I-TAKE-ADVANTAGE-HIM.   'I understand. I don't want to take advantage of him.'

_ t ___

3. READY, I HAPPY I-SUMMON-HER.   'When it's ready I'll be happy to call her.'

_____ t _____

4. HIS SCHEDULE I-COPY-HIM CAN I.   'I can copy his schedule.'

5. I WANT I-CHOOSE-HER.   'I would like to choose her.'

EXERCISE 15.2

_____ t _____

1. HER HOMEWORK YOU-COPY-HER.   'You copied her homework.'

_____ q _____

2. CAN YOU-TAKE-HIM THERE Z-O-O?   'Can you take him to the zoo?'

_____ t _____

3. YOU READY LEAVE, YOU-SUMMON-HIM.   'Now that you're ready to go, go get him.'

4. NOT LIKE YOU-TAKE-ADVANTAGE-HER. 'I don't like your taking advantage of her.'
5. SURPRISE YOU-CHOOSE-HIM PRESIDENT C-L-U-B. 'I'm surprised you elected him as president of the club.'

EXERCISE 15.3

YESTERDAY I I-TELL-THEM-TWO, RAIN WILL. 'I told the two of them that it would rain.'

___ t ___
2. MONEY HE-GIVE-TWO-THEM. 'He gave the two of them some money.'
3. BETTER YOU-ASK-TWO-THEM. SURE YOU RIGHT YOU. 'You had better ask the two of them. Be sure you are right.'
4. I WANT I-TAKE-YOU-TWO THERE RESTAURANT. 'I want to take both of you to the restaurant.'
5. YOU-PL. BEST, I WANT I-CHOOSE-YOU-TWO. 'You are the best, I want to pick both of you.'
6. BEER I-CL:C-GIVE-TWO-THEM. 'I gave the two of them some beer.'

_____ t ___
7. DAUGHTER I I-SEND-TWO-THEM LETTER WILL I. 'I'll send my two daughters a letter.'

EXERCISE 15.4

_ t _
1. THIEF COP FINISH HE-CATCH-EACH-OF-THEM. 'The cop caught each of the thiefs.'

_____ q _____
2. PLEASE FOR ME, CAN YOU YOU-ASK-ALL-OF-THEM? 'Could you please ask all of them for me?'
3. WANT I I-INVITE-EACH-OF-THEM MY WEDDING. 'I would like to invite each of them to my wedding.'
4. TOMORROW I I-INFORM-ALL-OF-YOU WHO WIN. 'I'll let you all know who won tomorrow.'

_____ t _____
5. MY OLD CLOTHES WILL I I-GIVE-ALL-OF-THEM. 'I'll give my old clothes to all of them.
6. FINISH I I-TELL-ALL-OF-YOU MUST YOU-PL. COME-HERE TIME 8. 'I already told all of you that you had to come here at 8 o'clock.'

_____ t _____
7. THEY CHILDREN MOTHER SHE-SEND-EACH-OF-THEM BOX. 'The mother sent each of the children a box.'

EXERCISE 16.1

1. MOVIE IT CONTINUE 3-HOUR. 'The movie lasted for three hours.'

_____ t _____
2. COURSE I TAKE-UP 8-WEEK. 'The course I'm taking is 8 weeks long.'
3. NOW TWO-US MARRY 7 YEAR. 'Now the two of us have been married for 7 years.'
4. FIVE-US PLAN GO-AWAY BACKPACKING MAYBE 5-DAY. 'The five of us plan to go backpacking for maybe 5 days.'
5. NOW LEFT 6-MONTH, MOVE-AWAY WILL I. 'Now there's only 6 months left then I'll be moving away.'
6. I ORDER BED NEW, I MUST WAIT 4-WEEK. 'I ordered a new bed and I have to wait 4 weeks for it.'
7. HE LOSE ALMOST 9-DAY. 'He was lost for almost 9 days.'

EXERCISE 16.2

1. F-R-A-T MEETING WILL HERE IN-FOUR-YEAR. 'There'll be a National Fraternal Society of the Deaf meeting here in 4 years.'

2. LAST TIME I I-SEE-YOU LAST-YEAR, RIGHT? 'The last time I saw you was last year, right?'
3. 25 YEAR PAST HARD FIND INTERPRETER. '25 years ago it was hard to find an interpreter.'
4. PARTY THERE MY HOME IN-THREE-MONTH. 'There'll be a party at my home in three months.'
5. I GO-THERE FINISH SIX-WEEK-AGO. 'I went there six weeks ago.'
6. HE GRADUATE GALLAUDET FOUR-YEAR-AGO. 'He graduated from Gallaudet four years ago.'
7. C-O SAY WILL BRING-HERE BED IN-FOUR-WEEK. 'The company said it would bring the bed in four weeks.'

EXERCISE 16.3

1. IT-SEND-ME NEWSPAPER MONTHLY. 'They send me a newspaper every month.'
2. MUST I TAKE-PILL DAILY. 'I must take a pill everyday.'
3. SHE GO-THERE EUROPE BUSINESS MONTHLY. 'She goes to Europe on business every month.'
4. SHE EXERCISE WEEKLY. 'She exercises every week.'
5. HE TO-TELEPHONE I DAILY, I BORED I. 'He calls me every day and I'm bored.'

DIALOGUE 5

Jane: I haven't seen you for awhile. I hear you have a new job. How is it?
Ron: It's fine. I'm the only Deaf person there. They don't know sign language. I decided to set up a sign language class. It's two hours on Tuesdays and Thursdays. Wow, things really improved.
Jane: That was a good idea. Does your boss sign and fingerspell?
Ron: A little bit. I have three bosses. I gave each of them a sign language book. They have learned a little. I should get a TTY next week. Then you can call me.
Jane: Great. Two weeks ago another Deaf person was added to my group, now we have six Deaf people working at my company. Will your company hire more Deaf people?
Ron: Probably.
Bill: Ready? The movie is starting now.

EXERCISE 17.1

        _____t _____ ____n _____
1. FINISH ADVERTISE TOURNAMENT, I DON'T-KNOW I. 'I don't know if they have advertised the tournament.'
        _____t _____ ____n ____
2. HE APPLY FOR PRESIDENT, HE DOUBT HE. 'He doubts he will apply for president.'
        _____t _____
3. TWO-THEM ARGUE ALL-DAY, TEND TWO-THEM. 'They tend to argue all day.'
        _____t _____ _____ y_____
4. I SUPPORT WHEELCHAIR, HE KNOW-THAT HE. 'He knows that I support the disabled.'
        _____t _____ ___n _____
5. BORROW MONEY FROM BOSS, SHE DON'T-WANT SHE. 'She doesn't want to borrow money from her boss.'
        ___t ____ __n ____
6. I AGAIN BROKE, I DON'T-WANT. 'I don't want to be broke again.'
        ____t _____
7. GO-BY-BOAT THERE EUROPE, THREE-US WANT. 'The three of us want to go to Europe by boat.'
        __t __ __n __
8. HE FIRED, NOT HE. 'He's not fired.'
        _____t _____ ___ y ___
9. HE GRANDFATHER TELL-STORY, HE LIKE HE. 'Grandfather likes to tell stories.'
        ____t _____ __n ____
10. STAY PARTY ALL-NIGHT, I DON'T-LIKE I. 'I don't like to stay at parties all night.'

EXERCISE 17.2

       _____t _____
1. HOUSE R-E-N-T, A-P-T R-E-N-T, IT WORSE IT.   'House rent is worse (higher) than apartment rent.'

       _____t _____
2. IT WOOD TABLE, IT METAL TABLE, I WANT IT.   'I want the wood table not the metal table.'

       _____t _____
3. STAY HOME WATCH T-V, GO-AWAY MOVIE PAY

      _____
    5-DOLLAR, IT BETTER IT.   'It is better to stay home and watch TV than to pay five dollars to see a movie.'

       _____t _____
4. IT FLOWER REAL, IT FLOWER S-I-L-K, IT PRETTIER IT.   'The real flower is prettier than the silk one.'

       _____t _____ _____q ____
5. IT EXPENSIVE, IT CHEAP, YOU WANT IT?   'Do you want the expensive one or the cheap one?'

       _____t _____
6. I GO-THERE COLLEGE, I STAY WORK, I STAY I.   'I decided to stay and work rather than go to college.'

       _____t _____
7. MEETING HERE, MEETING THERE, I PREFER IT.   'I prefer to meet here not there.'

EXERCISE 17.3

1. SHE RESEARCH A-S-L, HIT FIND RULE++.   'She was doing research on ASL, and it turned out that she found many rules.'
2. SHE GO-THERE BUY T-T-Y, HAPPEN S-A-L-E.   'She went to buy a TTY and it happened that there was a sale on them.'
3. BABY SEEM SICK, FIND HAVE EAR-ACHE.   'The baby seemed to be sick and then we found out that she had an ear ache.'
4. CLOTHES PUT-IN WASH-IN-MACHINE, FRUSTRATE RUIN.   'I put my clothes in the washing machine and to my dismay, they were ruined.'
5. I BUY GLASS NEW, WRONG DAMAGE.   'I had just bought a new glass when it was damaged.'
6. TWO-US CHAT, FIND SAME HAVE DEAF PARENTS.   'We were talking and then we found out that we both have deaf parents.'
7. I WATCH T-V, WRONG CAPTION.   'I was watching television when suddenly captions appeared (on the screen).'
8. I DRIVE-THERE, FRUSTRATE SHE NOT HOME.   'I drove there only to find her not at home.'
9. HE HAVE NEW CAR, FRUSTRATE STEAL.   'He had a new car then to his dismay, it was stolen.'
10. HE ACT NOTHING-TO-IT, WRONG SHOT-UP FAMOUS.   'He was performing in bit roles when all of a sudden, he hit it big and became famous.'

EXERCISE 18.1

1. YESTERDAY NIGHT I-TTY-YOU-REPEATEDLY (with effort), YOU NONE YOU.   'Last night I called you on the teletypewriter many times but you weren't there.'

       _____t _____
2. PITY-HIM, TEAM HIS LOUSY, HE LOSE-COMPETITION-REPEATEDLY (carelessly).   'I feel sorry for him—his team is so bad and they always lose so badly.'
3. BROTHER TEND ANALYZE-REPEATEDLY (with attention) MOVIE.   'My brother has a tendency to analyze a movie thoroughly.'

4. SHE BOTHER-HIM-REPEATEDLY (carelessly),
   WRONG HE-BAWL-OUT-HER. 'She kept bothering him heedlessly and then suddenly he bawled
                                              her out.'
                    __t __
5. HE THIRSTY. WATER HE DRINK-REPEATEDLY (with effort).
   'He was thirsty so he kept gulping down water.'
6. SHE LOVE READ-REPEATEDLY (with ease). 'She loves to just read and read.'
   _____ t ____
7. BASKETBALL, NEW-YORK BEFORE
   WIN-REPEATEDLY (with ease). 'New York used to win all their basketball games easily.'
8. FINISH I-WARN-YOU REPEATEDLY (with effort)
   SHOULD FIX T-I-R-E. 'I have warned you many times that you should fix that tire.'
9. BORED I-PRESENT-YOU-REPEATEDLY (with effort)
   MONEY. I'm tired of having to give you money all the time.'
10. FIND HE INFORM-HIM-REPEATEDLY (with attention
    POLICE. 'It was discovered that he had been diligently informing the police.'

EXERCISE 18.2

1. HE STAY-THERE-CONTINUALLY (with ease)
   3-HOUR FINISH COME-HERE. 'He lingered there for 3 hours then came back.'
2. HE APPEAR NONE, I WAIT-CONTINUALLY (with effort)
   'He didn't show up so I waited a long time.'
3. TRAVEL-AROUND, I WANT-CONTINUALLY (with effort).
   'I've always longed to travel.'
4. SHE EAT-CONTINUALLY (carelessly),
   WRONG BECOME-FAT. 'She kept eating carelessly and without realizing it she became fat.'
5. HARD UNDERSTAND HE FINGERSPELL-
   CONTINUALLY (with attenton). 'It's hard to understand him because he diligently fingerspells all
                                              the time.'
6. WOOD BURN-CONTINUALLY (with ease)
   3-HOUR. 'The wood burned steadily for 3 hours.'
7. HOMEWORK I STRUGGLE-CONTINUALLY (with effort),
   FINALLY I UNDERSTAND. 'I struggled mightily with my homework and finally I understood it.'

EXERCISE 19.1

1. K-A-N-S-A-S VERY-CL:BB. 'Kansas is very flat.'
2. WINTER THERE M-I-N-N VERY-COLD. 'The winters are very cold in Minnesota.'
3. HER HOME WOW VERY-SMALL. 'Her home is very small.'
4. SNOW ALL-OVER WOW VERY-WHITE. 'The snow covering everything was very white.'
5. YOUR LECTURE VERY-CLEAR. 'Your lecture was very clear.'
   _____ n _____
6. YOU WORK NOTHING, VERY-LAZY YOU. 'You haven't done a thing, you're so lazy.'
7. BASKETBALL PLAYER HE WOW VERY-TALL. 'The basketball player is very tall.'
8. GAS NOW VERY-EXPENSIVE. 'Gas is now very expensive.'
9. MUST YOU GO-THERE MEETING,
   IT VERY-IMPORTANT. 'You must go to the meeting, it is very important.'
   _____ t ____
10. RAIN SINCE, WOW VERY-WORSE. 'The rain we've been having is the worst ever.'

EXERCISE 19.2

                    _whq __
1. SHE MAD-REPEATEDLY. WRONG? 'What's wrong with her? She's mad all the time.'
2. FOOTBALL PLAYER HE HURT-REPEATEDLY. 'The football player keeps getting hurt.'

3. FATHER WORRY. I LATE-REPEATEDLY I.   'My father worries because I'm always late.'
   _____ n _____
4. SINCE DON'T-KNOW WHY,
   I SICK-REPEATEDLY.   'I don't know why but I keep getting sick.'
5. DOWNSTAIRS HAVE DOG,
   NOISE-REPEATEDLY AWFUL.   'There's a dog downstairs that keeps making terrible noises.'
   _____ n _____
6. HE JUDGMENT NONE,
   HE WRONG-REPEATEDLY.   'He's always making mistakes because he has no judgment.'
7. HE LOOK-FOR WORK,
   FRUSTRATE-REPEATEDLY HE.   'He is frustrated everywhere he looks for work.'

EXERCISE 19.3

1. LIKE I OUTSIDE SIT, LOOK-AT
   PEOPLE DIFFERENT-CONTINUALLY.   'I like to sit outside and look at all the different people.'
   _____ t _____
2. PARTY THERE, SHE EMBARRASSED-
   CONTINUALLY ALL-NIGHT.   'At the party she was continually embarrassed all night.'
   _____ n _____
3. I DON'T KNOW, SEEM I WRONG-
   CONTINUALLY.   'I don't know, it seems like I'm wrong all the time.'
4. HE BUY NEW CAR, SINCE
   CAREFUL-CONTINUALLY HE.   'Ever since he bought a new car he's been very careful with it.'
5. AUNT SICK-CONTINUALLY.
   WRONG LOST #JOB.   'My aunt was always sick and then she lost her job.'
6. ALL-DAY GIRL MISCHIEVOUS-CONTINUALLY.   'The girl was mischievous all day.'
   _____ t _____
7. CAPTION T-V HAVE DIFFERENT-CONTINUALLY.   'There are many different captioned TV shows.'

DIALOGUE 6

Don: In the past there were no teletypewriters, decoders, and interpreters like there are now. You young people have plenty of things.
Mary: When did you buy your first teletypewriter?
Don: Back in 1971.
Mary: How much did it cost?
Don: 60 dollars. Back then, teletypewriters were very big, now they're very small and cost 600 dollars.
Mary: Wow. It's worth having a teletypewriter.
Don: That's true. I remember once—I wanted to go and visit a friend; I had to drive to my friend's place. Sometimes I would drive there, and to my dismay, my friend wasn't there. I had to keep going back until I got ahold of my friend. I've been frustrated many times.
Mary: Now I just call up my friend on the teletypewriter and find that he's not home. I save my gas.
Don: That's true. Comparing the way things were in the past with the way they are now, it's better now.

EXERCISE 20.1

   _____ if _____
1. AIRPLANE AGAIN POSTPONE, I MAD I.   'If the plane is delayed again, I'll be mad.'
   _____ if _____
2. MONEY YOU-GIVE ME NOW, I BUY TICKET I.   'If you give me the money now, I can buy the ticket.'

_____ if _____
3. C-F I GET FINISH, I-INFORM-ALL-OF-YOU. 'If I get the captioned film, I'll let you all know.'
_____ if _____
4. YOU DRIVE-THERE, I GO-WITH WANT I. 'If you're driving there, I'd like to go with you.'
_____ if _____
5. T-V CAPTION HAVE HE, I GO-
THERE HIS HOME. 'If he has a decoder, I'll go to his home.'
_____ if _____
6. T-V HAVE ACTOR DEAF IT,
I WATCH MUST I. 'If there's a television show with a deaf actor, then I have to watch it.'
_____ if _____
7. LEARN SIGN HE WANT,
PRACTICE MUST HE. 'If he wants to learn to sign, he has to practice.'

EXERCISE 20.2

    _ rq _
1. THEY FINISH VOTE PRESIDENT C-L-U-B, WHO? BROTHER. 'They've elected a president for the club and who is it?? My brother.'
    ___ rq _____
2. NOW RESEARCH-REPEATEDLY SIGN, WHAT-FOR? UNDERSTAND LANGUAGE. 'Now they're doing a lot of research on sign language—why? To understand language.'
_ t _   ___ rq _
3. CAR I FINISH DECIDE BUY, WHICH? D-A-T-S-U-N. 'I've decided to buy a car—which one? A Datsun.'

    ___ rq _
4. HE LECTURE-REPEATEDLY, WHAT?
ABOUT C-L-E-R-C, HIMSELF DEAF. 'He frequently lectures on what? Clerc, who is deaf.'
5. I GO-THERE PUT-IN-GAS.
    ____ rq ____
HOW-MUCH? 20 DOLLAR. 'I went to get gas, and how much was it? 20 dollars.'
    _ rq _
6. YOU GO-TO-IT CLOSE-DOOR. WHY?
BUG ENTER-REPEATEDLY. 'Go and close the door. Why? Because the bugs keep coming in.'

EXERCISE 21.1

1. WOW VERY-BIG AIRPORT,
HAVE AIRPLANE CL:ᴛ-IN-A-ROW. 'Wow, it's an enormous airport; there's a whole row of airplanes.'
2. BEFORE NONE, NOW HAVE DEAF
BUSINESS CL:Å-ALL-OVER. 'Before there weren't any but now there are businesses run by Deaf people all over.'
3. I LOOK-AT, SEE BIRD CL:V̈-IN-A-ROW. 'I looked and saw some birds sitting in a row.'
4. ARMY READY, IT HAVE AIRPLANE
CL:ᴛ-IN-A-ROW. 'The military is prepared; they have airplanes lined up in a row.'
5. PARTY FINISH, WOW BEER CAN
CL:C-ALL-OVER. 'After the party, there were beer cans all over the place.'
    _____ t _____
6. NOW PRICE HIGH, CAR NEW CL:3-IN-A-ROW
CAN'T SELL. 'Now prices are high, they can't sell the row of new cars.'

266

7. BEER CAN FATHER ENJOY COLLECT.
   THERE HOME HAVE CL:C-IN-A-ROW.   'My father enjoys collecting beer cans. At home there's a
   row of cans.'

EXERCISE 21.2

       ___ n _____
1. CL:1(3)-THERE-TO-THERE, I SEE ~NONE.   'I didn't see the three of them pass by.'
2. GIRL CL:1(2)-THERE-TO-HERE CHAT FINISH,
   CL:1(2)-HERE-TO-THERE.   'The two girls came up to me, talked a bit, then left.'
3. BOY CL:1(5)-THERE-TO-HERE, DEMAND MONEY.
   I SHOCK. 'Five boys came up to me and demanded my money. I was stunned.'
4. BEAR CL:1(2)-THERE-TO-HERE,
   I HERE-RUN-THERE.   'Two bears came up to me, I ran in the opposite direction.'
   _____ q _____ _____ whq _____
5. CAN CL:1(4)-HERE-TO-THERE, ASK-HIM TIME MEETING WHAT?   'Can the four of us go up to
                                                                                 him and ask him what time
                                                                                  the meeting is?'

EXERCISE 21.3

   _____ y _____
1. HAVE LEFT CL:B.   'There's a lot left.'
     _____ y _____
   CL:B HAVE LEFT.   'There's a lot left.'
2. I HAVE CL:BB.   'I've got a big pile.'
   CL:BB I HAVE.   'I've got a big pile.'
     _____ y _____
3. I HAVE CL:BB.   'I've got a big pile of them.'
     _____ y _____
   CL:BB I HAVE.   'I've got a big pile of them.'
     ____ y _____
4. I FINISH TAKE CL:B.   'I already took a lot.'
     _____ y _____
   CL:B I FINISH TAKE.   'I already took a lot.'
     _____ y ____
5. SHE HAVE CL:44.   'She has a lot of them.'
     _____ y _____
   CL:44 SHE HAVE.   'She has a lot of them.'
6. CL:44 WANT BUY TICKET.   'There's a lot of people who want to buy tickets.'
     _____ y _____
7. IT HAVE CL:BB.   'They have a big pile of them.'
     ____ y _____
   CL:BB IT HAVE.   'They have a big pile of them.'

EXERCISE 22.1

1. OUTLINE-DINNER BELL-TRIANGULAR-SHAPED.
2. OUTLINE-HEADBOARD-BED.
3. OUTLINE-SWIMMING-POOL-L-SHAPED.
4. OUTLINE-COIL-OR-SPRING.
5. OUTLINE-LEAF.
6. OUTLINE-HEARTBEAT-MONITOR.
7. OUTLINE-CLOSED-CAPTIONING-SYMBOL.

EXERCISE 22.2

1. SHAPE-ARABIAN-TENT.
2. SHAPE-ROAD-THAT-ENDS-ABRUPTLY-AT-A-DROPOFF.
3. SHAPE-WRINKLED-CARPET.
4. SHAPE-ICY-SURFACE.
5. SHAPE-STAIRS
6. SHAPE-CHINESE-WOK.
7. SHAPE-MOUNTAIN-RANGE.

EXERCISE 22.3

1. BEFORE I WORK FACTORY COKE CL:44⇉. 'I used to work in a coke factory on an assembly line.'

   BEFORE I WORK FACTORY CAN CL:44⇉. 'I used to work in a can factory on an assembly line.'

   BEFORE I WORK FACTORY FISH CL:44⇉. 'I used to work in a fish factory on an assembly line.'

   BEFORE I WORK FACTORY CAR CL:44⇉. 'I used to work in an auto factory on an assembly line.'

2. MEETING IMPORTANT DEAF CL:55⇅. 'A lot of Deaf people came to the important meeting.'

   MEETING IMPORTANT COP CL:55⇅. 'A lot of cops came to the important meeting.'

   MEETING IMPORTANT INTERPRETER CL:55⇅. 'A lot of interpreters came to the important meeting.'

   MEETING IMPORTANT RESEARCHER CL:55⇅. 'A lot of researchers came to the important meeting.'

3. #BUSY HE DAILY STUDENT CL:44⇉ HIS ROOM. 'He is so busy, everyday students keep filing into his office.'

   #BUSY HE DAILY SICK PEOPLE CL:44⇉ HIS ROOM. 'He is so busy, everyday sick people keep filing into his office.'

   #BUSY HE DAILY ACTOR CL:44⇉ HIS ROOM. 'He is so busy, everyday actors keep filing into his office.'

   #BUSY HE DAILY BOY, GIRL CL:44⇉ HIS ROOM. 'He is so busy, everyday boys and girls keep filing into his office.'

4. AWFUL ALL-NIGHT #GAS CL:4↓. 'It was awful, the gas had been leaking all night.'

   AWFUL ALL-NIGHT NOSE CL:4↓. 'It was awful, my nose had been running all night.'

   AWFUL ALL-NIGHT TOILET CL:4↓. 'It was awful, the toilet had been leaking all night.'

   AWFUL ALL-NIGHT ROOF CL:4↓. 'It was awful, the roof had been leaking all night.'

DIALOGUE 7

Jack: I got a television decoder last week. It's really wonderful.

Alice: I have ordered one. I'm still waiting; it hasn't arrived. What does it look like?

Jack: It has a flat top, is about this long, and it's made of metal. It has a channel knob. If there is a captioned show on television, you set it on "Caption" and the captions will appear.

Alice: They made some decoders but then they had a run on the market. They did not expect that. Now they are starting to produce and sell more.

Jack: Do you know how the decoder works? The television screen is made up of several horizontal lines, one of which is line 21. That one has the caption signal. You must have a box, the television decoder, which you plug in to make the captions appear.

Alice: That's really wonderful. I can't wait to get mine.

VOCABULARY INDEX

sign language 31
SIGN 31
SILLY 201
similar 130
simultaneously 163
SINCE 154
since 207
SISTER 20
SIT 96
SKI 142
SKIING 142
SKILL 87
skilled 220
SLEEP 106
SLEEPY 11
SLOW 107
SMALL 11
small 10
SMART 11
smart 141
SMELL 42
SNOW 142
so 43
socialize 152
SOFT 78
SOME 142
someone 184
SOMETHING 184
SOMETIMES 142
SON 20
song 191
SOPHISTICATED 174
SORRY 43
soul 222
sound 41
soup 78
SOUR 191
SOUTH 184
SPAIN 232
Spanish 232
speak 119
SPECIAL 222
speech 10, 105

SPEND 154
SPIRIT 222
split 208
spoiled 183
sponsor 184
SPOON 78
SPORTS 104
spring 66
STAMP 78
STAND 192
START 174
STAY 54
STEADY-DATE 184
steak 65
STEAL 96
STILL 78
STOP 96
STOP-IT 78
STORE 78
STORY 96
STRANGE 143
STREET 130
strength 11
stress 190
STRICT 130
STRONG 11
STRUGGLE 192
STUDENT 20
STUDY 87
STUPID 11
stupid 9
sub-titles 181
SUBTRACT 211
SUCCEED 163
succeed 162
success 163
sue 210
SUGAR 66
suggest 163
SUITCASE 88
SUMMARIZE 222
SUMMER 96
SUMMON 163

SUN 130
SUNDAY 67
SUNRISE 130
SUNSET 130
superintendent 106
SUPERVISE 222
supper 75
SUPPORT 184
SUPPOSE 201
SUPPRESS 201
sure 153
surgery 221
SURPRISED 11
surrender 173
SWALLOW 201
swear 129
SWEET 67
sweet 66
switch 208, 222
sympathy 174
TABLE 31
TAKE 163
TAKE-ADVANTAGE-OF
   163
take out 163
TAKE-PICTURE 154
TAKE-PILL 174
TAKE-UP 107
talk with 29
TALK 119
TALL 11
TASTE 43
tax 142
TEA 67
TEACH 20
TEACHER 20
TEAM 192
team 29
TELEPHONE 97
TELETYPEWRITER 67
TELL 67
TELL-STORY 96
TEMPERATURE 201

WHITE 31

WHITE PERSON 31

WHO 89

WHY 89

why 88

WIFE 20

WILL 54

WIN 107

WINDOW 95

WINE 143

WINTER 40

wish 41

WITH 143

WOMAN 20

WONDER 222

WONDERFUL 97

won't 106

WOOD 184

WORD 43

work out 151

WORK 43

WORLD 43

WORRY 89

WORSE 164

worth it 119

worth 140

WOW 97

WRENCH 154

WRIST-WATCH 67

write down 106

WRITE 54

WRONG 43, 184

YEAR 54

YELLOW 31

YES 43

YESTERDAY 54

YOU 12

YOUNG 43

YOU-PL 12

YOUR 20

YOUR-PL 20

yours 20

YOURSELF 89

YOURSELVES 89

youth 43